Duns Scotus:

THE BASIC PRINCIPLES
OF HIS PHILOSOPHY

DUNS SCOTUS:

THE BASIC PRINCIPLES
OF HIS PHILOSOPHY

by Efrem Bettoni, O.F.M., Ph.D.
SCHOOL OF PHILOSOPHY
UNIVERSITY OF THE SACRED HEART,
MILAN

Translated and Edited

by Bernardine Bonansea, O.F.M., Ph.D.
SCHOOL OF PHILOSOPHY
THE CATHOLIC UNIVERSITY OF AMERICA

THE CATHOLIC UNIVERSITY OF AMERICA PRESS
Washington 17, D. C.
1961

Translator's Preface

NEED HAS LONG BEEN FELT for a concise and simple exposition of Duns Scotus' philosophical thought, in which the basic principles of his system would be presented against their doctrinal background, and the characteristic features of his speculation would be properly illustrated from the viewpoint of his new and original philosophical synthesis.

Father Efrem Bettoni, professor of philosophy at Sacred Heart University in Milan, and a recognized authority in the field of Scotistic studies, has successfully answered this need. His investigation of Duns Scotus' thought, which appears now for the first time in English translation, is an excellent study of the Scotistic system. In it clarity of exposition is matched by deep and penetrating analysis. One could hardly ask for a better presentation of the philosophy of Duns Scotus in a work of the proportions of the present one.

In undertaking the translation of Father Bettoni's work, I have had two main purposes in mind. First, to provide the English-speaking student of philosophy with a subsidiary work for a deeper knowledge of Duns Scotus' thought, which the ordinary textbooks usually present in a very superficial and inadequate way; second, to foster the study of one of the greatest figures of scholastic philosophy. Duns Scotus well deserves the title of *Doctor Subtilis*, not only because of his exact and penetrating distinctions, but most of all because of the power of his mind and the depth of his doctrine.

In certain respects the present translation can be considered an improvement upon the original Italian text. The chapters on the life and works of Duns Scotus have been revised and brought up to date in the light of recent studies and discoveries. Each chapter has been divided into sections, and occasionally the sections have been divided into paragraphs. All the references have been carefully checked against Scotus' original works and certain corrections have been made. Many additional footnotes have been inserted whenever it has seemed necessary to clarify particular points. These new notes are marked by asterisks and/or brackets to distinguish them from those in the original Italian text. Because of the many important Scotistic studies that have appeared since 1946, the year of publication of Father Bettoni's work, the bibliography has been greatly enlarged. This has been done especially with a view to the needs of the English-speaking student. An analytic index has also been added. Finally, care has been given to the printing and format of the work.

It is the translator's hope that this work will be of help to students of philosophy who desire a better understanding of a system that has played so important a role in the development of scholastic thought and has won the admiration of so many philosophers even outside the scholastic field.

The translator wishes to take this opportunity to express his sincere gratitude to the Right Reverend Msgr. John K. Ryan, Ph.D., Dean of the School of Philosophy, the Catholic University of America, and to the Reverend Ignatius Brady, O.F.M., Ph.D., Associate Professor of Philosophy in the same University, for their reading of the manuscript and their helpful suggestions which have contributed greatly to improve the text of the present translation. He extends his thanks also to Rev. Kieran Kemner, O.F.M., and Mr. Paul I. Seman, who went over the manuscript and suggested further improvements, and especially to Miss Elisabeth A. Murawski, editorial assistant of the Catholic University of America Press, for her constant efforts and technical supervision in the publication of this book.

TABLE OF CONTENTS

PART ONE

THE MAN AND HIS WORKS

PART TWO

DUNS SCOTUS' THOUGHT

PART THREE

DUNS SCOTUS IN HISTORY AND
CATHOLIC THOUGHT

PART ONE
THE MAN AND HIS WORKS

I

LIFE

THE CARELESSNESS of medieval writers with regard to biographical data and psychological observations serving to catch the personality of a master as he was in actual life is particularly noticeable in the case of John Duns Scotus. Historical material on the Subtle Doctor was at one time so scarce and vague that doubts were cast even on his existence. Some went so far as to consider him a mere symbol, the banner of a philosophical school. Today, after painstaking research, certain definite biographical facts have been ascertained. On the basis of such data it is possible to present, by means of inference and reflection, a fairly accurate historical account of Duns Scotus' life.[1]

John Duns Scotus was born in Scotland either at Maxton-on-Tweed, in the county of Roxburgh, on an estate still known as Littledean, or, as most recent discoveries seem to indicate,

---

[1] The documentation of the content of this chapter can be found in the first part of my work, *Vent'anni di studi scotisti* (Milan: Vita e Pensiero, 1943). [This chapter has been revised and brought up to date on the basis of the author's more recent article on Duns Scotus in *Enciclopedia Filosofica* (Venice-Rome: Istituto per la Collaborazione Culturale, 1957), vol. IV, cols. 463-472, under *Scoto*, Giovanni Duns. *(Translator's note.)*]

at Duns, in the county of Berwick. The opinion, based on the authority of Luke Wadding, which claims for Ireland the glory of being the birthplace of the great medieval master, now has been definitely discarded.

The exact date of Scotus' birth is not known. However, all biographers agree in placing it between December 23, 1265, and March 17, 1266. His father was called Ninian Duns of Littledean. The Duns family had always been among the benefactors of the Friars Minor from the first arrival of the Order in Scotland. A member of this family, the paternal uncle of Duns Scotus, joined the Order and took the name of Father Elias Duns. It is little wonder, then, that a new Franciscan vocation matured in such a favorable environment.

In 1278, Father Elias Duns was appointed Vicar General of the Friars Minor of Scotland by a chapter which held its meeting at Haddington. At the time, John Duns was a boy of twelve or thirteen in this Scottish town. He was then attending its grammar school, where he first gave proof of his remarkable talents and piety.

One of the first acts of the new Vicar General was to accept his nephew for the Order, since he had every sign of a vocation. He brought him to the friary of Dumfries, where he himself was stationed, in order to help him prepare for his definite entrance into the Order. Since Duns Scotus was at the time not yet fifteen, the age required by the constitutions of the Order for the reception of novices, this ceremony must have taken place towards the end of 1280.

The date of his ordination to the priesthood at the hands of Oliver Sutton, bishop of Lincoln, is known for sure. It took place on March 17, 1291, when Duns Scotus was twenty-five years old, at St. Andrew's, a church entrusted to the Monks of Cluny. However, no reliable information has come down to us as to the place of his studies between 1281 and 1291 in preparation for the priesthood. The statements of some historians, that he spent those years at Oxford, where there was a flourishing

Studium Generale of the Friars Minor close to the University, opened under the protection and at the instigation of Robert Grosseteste, are not supported by any historical document. The well-known Scotist, Father Ephrem Longpré, seems to have good reasons to believe that, in addition perhaps to his temporary residence at Oxford, Duns Scotus spent a few years at Paris between 1283 and 1290. This would explain more naturally Scotus' familiarity with the writings of Giles of Rome, Godfrey of Fontaines, and especially Henry of Ghent, all professors at Paris during that period. In this case, it would also have been possible for him to become personally acquainted with Richard of Middleton, Peter John Olivi, and Gonsalvus of Spain, and to be influenced by them in the formation of his thought. At any rate, all historians accept as definitely established the fact that Scotus was at Paris between 1294 and 1297. In that city he perfected himself in the study of philosophy and theology.

It is known with certainty that in 1302 the Subtle Doctor was commenting, as a bachelor, on the *Sentences* of Peter Lombard at the University of Paris. However, the Scotistic tradition is unanimous in affirming that Duns Scotus commented on the *Sentences* at Oxford even before he did so in Paris. This tradition is acceptable and not difficult to confirm. Indeed, it is more than reasonable to think that, before exposing the young master to the judgment and criticism of the University of Paris, his superiors wished to be sure of his teaching ability and scientific preparation. Thus it can be assumed that Duns Scotus had already revealed his exceptional qualities both as a scholar and as a teacher in one of the Order's houses of study. Nothing prevents us from believing that this was the *Studium Generale* in Oxford. In addition to Paris and Oxford, Duns Scotus also taught at Cambridge.

In 1304 Duns Scotus was already known both within and outside the Order as a religious of deep spirituality and as a man of wide culture and powerful mind. When Father Gon-

salvus of Spain, Minister General of the Franciscan Order, proposed him to the Provincial of Paris as a candidate for a master's chair at the University of that city, he expressed himself
in the following terms: "I recommend to your charity our beloved brother in Christ, Father John Scotus, whose laudable
life, excellent knowledge, most subtle genius, and other remarkable qualities are fully known to me, partly because of
my long association with him, and partly because of his wide-
spread reputation."

However, in 1304 Duns Scotus was no longer in Paris, as
he had to leave the city suddenly in 1303, in the middle of the
academic year. What was the reason for this sudden departure?
In the first months of 1303 the struggle between Pope Boniface VIII and the King of France, Philip the Fair, which is
better known from Dante's poem (cf. *Purgatorio,* XX, 85-93)
than from the reports of historians, had become greatly in-
tensified. Philip the Fair looked for adherents to his antipapal
policies among the clergy. This led to a split even among the
members of the religious orders. Duns Scotus, as is well documented by the list of the Friars Minor that took side with
the Pope against the King—a list discovered and published
by Father Ephrem Longpré in 1928—did not hesitate to follow
the dictates of conscience and truth. Royal reprisal forced him
to interrupt his teaching and return to Oxford in England,
where he lectured during the scholastic year 1303-1304.

When in 1304, following the death of Boniface VIII, the
storm subsided and all political difficulties were removed, John
Duns Scotus was sent back to Paris by the Minister General
in order to obtain the title of master. About Easter in 1305,
when Simon of Guiberville was chancellor of the University,
the official proclamation took place.

This second period of teaching at the University of Paris
became famous in scholastic tradition because of the theological dispute of the Subtle Doctor in favor of the Immaculate Conception of the Blessed Mother. Later traditions have

invested this famous battle with legendary elements. Allegedly it ended in a grand finale, in which the Franciscan master, emulating in the field of culture the deeds of the bravest knights, victoriously withstood all the masters of the University of Paris, who were fierce opponents of his Mariology. However, the substantial historicity of this famous dispute has been proved in recent years by Father Charles Balic with an abundance of arguments which show how well Duns Scotus deserves the title of knight as well as of doctor of the Immaculate Conception.*

By the beginning of the academic year 1307-1308 the Subtle Doctor was no longer stationed in Paris. His place there was taken by another Franciscan, Father Alexander of Alexandria. In the first months of 1308, Duns Scotus was certainly in Cologne, where he lectured in the Franciscan House of Studies of the city. What are the reasons for this sudden departure from Paris where his teaching had commanded respect and admiration? In 1307, by order of Philip the Fair, Nogaret was preparing the famous process against the Knights Templar, which would once more place the King of France in opposition to the Pope. It was extremely important, if not necessary, for the University to show on such an occasion its solidarity with the royal house. Hence the precaution was taken of dismissing from the University those masters whose behavior clearly indicated their opposition to the intrigues of the French jurists. Duns Scotus was one of those masters. The precedent of 1303 could not leave any doubt as to his attitude. To add to this, his teaching on the Immaculate Conception of Mary offered to his opponents a good pretext to accuse him of heresy and have him removed, or even stand trial. An indication that things might have turned out this

---

* See P. Carolus Balic, O.F.M., "Ioannes Duns Scotus et Historia Immaculatae Conceptionis," *Antonianum*, XXX (1955), 349-488. This scholarly and authoritative article contains abundant information on the subject. *(Tr.)*

way for the Subtle Doctor is the *Quodlibet* of John of Pouilly, published in 1308. In it the theological thesis favoring the Immaculate Conception is characterized as heretical. Against those who defend it, it is further stated in the *Quodlibet* that "one must proceed not with arguments, but *otherwise*." If we reflect that John of Pouilly, a Frenchman, was a supporter of Philip the Fair, it will not be difficult to understand the kind of threatening atmosphere that was forming around the Marian Doctor.

The Minister General, Gonsalvus of Spain, who had a great love and appreciation for Scotus, and who had become acquainted with the situation in Paris during his many years of residence and teaching at the University, was no doubt concerned over the threats directed against the Scottish master. To save him from the approaching storm, the best expedient was to call him to Cologne, where he could be very helpful in the reorganization of the Franciscan *Studium* of that city and where he might be able to contribute to the intensification of the fight against the Beghards, whose heresy had a certain number of followers among the people of those regions. Thus, because of his devotion to the Pope and his love for the Blessed Mother, Duns Scotus was forced once more to leave the great theological center at Paris, the spiritual homeland of all great thirteenth-century masters.

In Cologne Duns Scotus had but one year of intensive work, for on November 8, 1308, he died prematurely at the age of forty-two or forty-three. On his tomb at Cologne there was engraved a Latin couplet:

> *Scotia me genuit—Anglia me suscepit,*
> *Gallia me docuit—Colonia me tenet.*

It is almost a historical synthesis of his life.

The glory of Duns Scotus' doctrine is matched by the glory of the sanctity of his life. His process of beatification was started in 1706. Difficulties of many kinds have been the cause

of delay in his glorification. However, a solemn petition for
the beatification of Duns Scotus was presented by the Franciscan Order to the Holy See in 1905, with the support of
more than 500 patriarchs, archbishops and bishops, 18 cardinals, and ten generals of religious orders. Both within the Franciscan Order and outside of it, there is hope that this petition
will be favorably acted upon by the Holy See.

II

WORKS

THE LITERARY patrimony of John Duns Scotus has not yet been critically established.[2] A special commission of scholars within the Order of Friars Minor, headed by Father Charles Balic, has been active during recent years in preparing a critical edition of Scotus' *Opera Omnia*. The first five volumes have already appeared in the following order: vols. I-II, 1950; vol. III, 1954; vol. IV, 1956; vol. V, 1959, all published by the Vatican City Press. Vol. I contains a *Disquisitio critica* and the *Prologus* to the *Ordinatio Prima,* the title given by Duns Scotus to his own compilation of the *Opus Oxoniense,* or commentary on the *Book of Sentences.* The other volumes contain Scotus' commentary on the first *Distinctiones* of the first book of the *Sentences.* Thus far, the most complete and reliable edition of Scotus' works is still Luke Wadding's edition printed at Lyons in 1639 (reprinted by Vivès in the final years of the last cen-

---

[2] The second part of my bibliographical essay, *Vent'anni di studi scotisti, op. cit.,* contains a faithful report on the conclusions reached by the scholars on Duns Scotus' literary patrimony. In this chapter, I follow the general lines of that report. [The content of this chapter has also been checked against the author's article in *Enciclopedia Filosofica.* See above n. 1. *(Tr.)*]

tury) together with the commentaries of the best Scotists of
the fifteenth and sixteenth centuries.

The Vivès edition consists of 26 folio volumes and includes
27 works. Some of these are authentic, while others are either
apocryphal or of doubtful authenticity. For practical purposes,
I will omit in this study all Scotus' unpublished writings and
mention only the works contained in the Vivès edition.

AUTHENTIC WORKS

1. Short works which can be grouped under the title of
Logic of Scotus. They make up a large part of the first two
volumes of the Vivès edition.

2. *Quaestiones in libros Aristotelis De Anima* (Vivès ed.,
vol. III). This work is incomplete. The *Supplementum* was
written by the seventeenth-century Scotist Hugo Cavello, and
is not always a faithful interpretation of the Master's thought.

3. *De Primo Principio* (Vivès ed., vol. IV), a short but
valuable work, which is a wonderful, profound exposition of
the Scotistic theodicy. It is also very important because it reveals the mystical character of Scotus' speculation. Here bold
speculation so mingles with fervent prayer, that Scotus ranks
high with such great masters as St. Augustine, St. Anselm,
and St. Bonaventure. However, it is difficult to read, not only
for beginners, but for others as well, because of the conciseness
and depth of the argumentation, impregnated as it is with
metaphysical thought.

4. *Collationes* (Vivès ed., vol. V). These are divided into
two groups, *Collationes Oxonienses* and *Collationes Parisienses,*
and have no particular importance.

5. *Quaestiones subtilissimae in Metaphysicam Aristotelis*
(Vivès ed., vol. VII), a work of Duns Scotus' youth, very
helpful for the study of the formation, and, to a certain extent,
of the evolution of Scotistic thought. The first nine books are
certainly authentic; the eleventh book is missing, and the tenth

and twelfth books are of doubtful authenticity. A reading of
these questions, where the main controversial metaphysical
problems of the time are discussed, is indispensable for anyone
who wishes to make a serious study of Duns Scotus' philosophy.

6. *Opus Oxoniense* (Vivès ed., vols. VIII-XXI). This is the
most important work of the Subtle Doctor. Here his thought
is displayed in its full extent and brilliancy. Although its
literary form is substantially that of a commentary on the
Sentences of Peter Lombard, it is as important for the knowledge of Scotus' thought as the *Summa Theologiae* is for the
knowledge of St. Thomas'. In reality, the *Opus Oxoniense* is
not merely the written compilation of a course given at the
University of Oxford, as the name might induce us to believe;
it is Scotus' definitive work and masterpiece.

The Subtle Doctor did not comment on the *Sentences* of
Peter Lombard only once; he commented on them several
times. Thus the first two books were commented upon by him
at least four times, the third book three times, and the fourth
book twice. All these university lectures exist in the form of
notes which, according to the custom of the time, were either
written by Duns Scotus himself, or taken down by his disciples and then revised by the Master. Most of these notes or
reports, known by the name of *Reportationes,* are still unpublished. But the work that has come down in tradition by the
name of *Opus Oxoniense,* even though it is written in the form
of a commentary, does not represent merely the actual content
of Scotus' teaching. It is a definitive work, which he compiled
and organized as time went on by putting together the best
of his lectures and giving final shape to his thought. Hence
the names of *Ordinatio* or *Liber Scoti* have been given to what
we call today the *Opus Oxoniense,* or Oxford Commentary.

Unfortunately, the Subtle Doctor was struck down by death
before he could finish his work. It is true that the main part
of it was done, but certain questions had scarcely been outlined,
while others were no more than scattered notes on the sub-

ject. Moreover, the margins of the manuscript are full of references, additions, and corrections. The work was completed by his disciples, who, instead of editing the Master's manuscript with all its lacunae and deficiencies, as would be done today, followed the system of the time and tried to make it appear as complete and perfect as possible. Thus a family of codices was born, to the extent that it was no longer possible to distinguish the genuine pages of Scotus from the changes made by his disciples.

As was to be expected, not everybody was satisfied with such subjective completions of the Master's thought. Attempts were made to re-establish the truth by distinguishing between Scotus' original writing and the additions of his disciples. Certain codices of the *Opus Oxoniense* written according to this criterion are now known to us. They are extremely important for the restoration of the *Ordinatio* to its original form, i.e., as it had been left by Scotus himself. This is the purpose of the critical edition now well under way. Let us hope that success attends the work of the editors.

Lack of a critical text of Scotus' main work does not prevent substantial knowledge of Scotus' doctrine, as some scholars seem to believe. This is particularly true of his philosophical thought. In fact, as all historians of medieval philosophy tell us, the thirteenth-century masters used to expound their philosophical doctrines almost exclusively in the first two books of their commentaries on the *Sentences*. At Duns Scotus' death, the first two books of the *Opus Oxoniense* were almost completed, and they are the most homogeneous and dependable of the books. On the other hand, Scotus dealt with philosophical problems in other treatises, also of a predominantly philosophical character. Hence, the comparison of his thought as it stands in the *Opus Oxoniense* with the same thought as we find it in his other writings is for us an almost absolute criterion for the authenticity of Scotus' doctrines. Finally, the logical consistency proper to any philosophical speculation worthy of the name is also a guide that cannot be disregarded in the interpretation of certain inaccuracies and lacunae found in the defective text at hand.

Whatever their value, these considerations are far from being an attempt to diminish the importance of the critical edition, which will no doubt help reconstruct Duns Scotus' philosophical thought on a more solid and sure basis. Their aim is simply to show that even if at the present time it is not yet possible to use critically established texts for studies of Scotist doctrine, the texts at hand are sufficiently reliable to depend upon.

7. *Reportata Parisiensia* (Vivès ed., vols. XXII-XXIV). This is another commentary on the *Sentences* of Peter Lombard compiled by Scotus' students. As such, it should reflect the Master's teaching at Paris. Wadding's text of the *Reportata* is differently evaluated by medievalists. However, they are one in saying that it is not completely reliable, and should therefore be used with greater caution than the text of the *Opus Oxoniense*. Because of its prevailingly theological character, the *Reportata* need not be considered as one of the primary sources for the study of Scotus' philosophy.

8. *Quodlibetum* (Vivès ed., vols. XXV-XXVI). If Wadding is to be believed, this is Scotus' last work. In addition to this, the twenty-one questions that make up the *Quodlibetum* constitute a very good source of study of Scotus' thought, for, as Wadding states in his *Praefatio,* the doctrines are therein expounded "more clearly, more methodically, and with more solid arguments." Hence, whenever an interpretation of the Subtle Doctor's thought can be supported with a passage from the *Quaestiones Quodlibetales,* there will be little doubt as to its dependence and reliability.

UNAUTHENTIC WORKS

Of the works contained in the Wadding-Vivès edition, the following are not authentic:

1. *Quaestiones in libros Physicorum Aristotelis* (Vivès ed., vols. II-III).
2. *Meteorologicorum libri quattuor* (Vivès ed., vol. IV).
3. *Quaestiones de rerum Principio* (Vivès ed., vol. IV).
4. *Quaestiones miscellaneae de formalitatibus* (Vivès ed., vol. V). Questions 2, 3, 4, 5 and 6 are certainly apocryphal.
5. *Metaphysicae textualis libri XII* (Vivès ed., vols. V, VI).
6. *Conclusiones Metaphysicae* (Vivès ed., vol. VI).

DOUBTFUL WORKS

The authenticity of the following works is still under discussion:

1. *Tractatus imperfectus de cognitione Dei* (Vivès ed., vol. V). More probably it is not authentic.
2. *De perfectione Statuum* (Vivès ed., vol. XXVI).
3. *Theoremata* (Vivès ed., vol. V). The authenticity of this opuscule has been strongly and heatedly debated. Thus far, no decisive arguments have been advanced either pro or con, and further study is needed.

Generally speaking, Scotus' works are very difficult to read. The task may even be discouraging. Such difficulty is due, in our opinion, to the following reasons. First, it must be admitted that by nature Duns Scotus is not as clear a writer as is, for example, St. Thomas Aquinas or St. Bonaventure. This serious disadvantage is aggravated by the confused state in which his works, and especially his major work, were handed down to us in manuscript form. Yet, in spite of the Subtle Doctor's dry and abstract style, many of the tortuous passages and syntactical lacunae that we find in his writings are doubtless due to the fact that he did not have the time to give them a finishing touch. They were thus left to the arbitrary handling of amanuenses.

A large part of the difficulty encountered in reading Scotus' works is also due to another factor. The student of medieval philosophy usually approaches the *Opus Oxoniense* after having made his acquaintance with the works of St. Thomas and St. Bonaventure. Now, for him who is used to the clear schematic structure of the Thomistic or Bonaventurian *quaestio,* there can be only disappointment and difficulty when he faces a question in the *Opus Oxoniense,* since he will find it so much more involved and confusing. Duns Scotus, for example, does not confine himself to a summary exposition of arguments pro and con. He subjects to critical evaluation the main solutions, if any, of the problem under discussion. He shows their weak points and stresses the need of a new solution. This will be his own solution, which he amply expounds in the *respondeo.* It will then be easy for him to prove that his own solution makes up for the deficiencies of other opinions and eventually reconciles all the different points of view.

Thus the scholastic *quaestio* becomes a treatise in its own right. The historical aspect of the problem is given more emphasis, but it becomes increasingly difficult to follow the logical thread hidden under the dialectical apparatus. Is this a sufficient reason for charging a thinker with obscurity and excessive subtlety? It does not seem so. Mere defects of forms and technique do not detract from the intrinsic value of a doctrine. If this value is not easy to discover, we are nevertheless rewarded for our efforts, for we shall find that we have at hand all the necessary elements for an objective evaluation of the doctrine in question.

III

THE GENESIS AND SPIRIT OF THE
SCOTISTIC SYNTHESIS

THE LAST thirty years of the thirteenth century were characterized by the conflict of the two philosophical schools that
had gradually taken shape within the Christian tradition: the
Augustinian school, which had found its most powerful and
homogeneous formulation in the works of St. Bonaventure;
and the Aristotelian school, created, rather than renewed, by
the penetrating genius of St. Thomas Aquinas. However we
may evaluate their differences, the existence of this conflict is
historically undeniable. While both schools agree in maintaining and defending the strict metaphysical transcendence
of God over creatures, they part company when the nature
and modes of the relationship between creatures and God are
to be determined.

Creation is the product of God's intelligence and love; all
things must therefore carry within themselves the vestiges
and the image of divine perfections. On the other hand, by
creating things distinct from Himself, God does not abandon
them; He keeps them in existence by the continuation of His
action on them. We must, then, discover in things the sign
of this divine collaboration. Finally, God created the world

15

for His own glory; He placed in all things an essential demand for their Creator, a profound stimulus that brings everything back to Him. What is the nature of this profound law of beings, whereby God is the final end of creation? How does it reveal itself to us? These are the concerns of the Augustinian school.

To state the problem more briefly: metaphysical transcendence does not exclude a certain immanence of God in things, especially in man. Indeed, only such an immanence furnishes a foundation for the return of things to God and makes it possible.

What, then, are the modes and manifestations in creatures of this divine transcendence? Augustinians are of the opinion that the Aristotelian school, concerned as it is with safeguarding divine transcendence, carries too far the distinction between the divine and the human element in things by attributing to creatures an excessive autonomy in respect to their Creator. In their view, the Aristotelians reduce almost to nothing the divine immanence in things as well as in man, and in so doing they seem to jeopardize the need and the possibility of their return to God.

Although in the disputes between Augustinians and Aristotelians preoccupations of a different order came to the surface, it is here, in our opinion, that the heart of the whole controversy must be sought. This is the position that lies at the bottom of all discussions; from it all the contrasting theses receive light and unity.[3]

It is not without reason that one of the doctrines the Augustinians defended most vigorously is precisely the theory of divine illumination. The return of things to God is effected

---

[3] This conviction has been formed in me from reading and meditating on St. Bonaventure and Duns Scotus, rather than from the consideration of more or less explicit texts of Augustinian works of the time. I shall have the opportunity to explain my thought more clearly in the course of this study.

through the intellect and will of man. It is through divine illumination that man has an innate idea of God and an indestructible desire for the supreme good, which give to man's faculties an opening on the infinite and create in them an urge that directs and stimulates man's ascent to God. This ascent is not sufficiently explained or safeguarded by Aristotle's empirical ideology. How could God be the supreme truth and supreme good for us, if there were not in man so deep-rooted an appeal to the infinite taking concrete form and finding expression in the psychological effects of divine illumination?

One should not forget that the adversaries of the Aristotelian "novelties" were not only Franciscan masters, but the great majority of the masters of theology, including many Dominicans. Until the end of the thirteenth century, to say the least, the doctrines of the Augustinian school were called *communes,* i.e., common doctrines. On the other hand, it was not without a certain amount of concern that the Holy See watched the development of the Aristotelian school. This is enough to show that the official doctrine of Rome was at the time the Augustinian doctrine. An objective study of the history of philosophy cannot help bearing witness to this fact. Indeed, from Gregory X, who was elected Supreme Pontiff in 1271, until Honorius IV, who died in 1287, all the popes had been, before their election, masters of the University of Paris. Moreover, they all manifested definitely, both in their writings and in official acts, their adherence to the Augustinian school.

An evident indication of the doctrinal trend prevailing in the Roman Curia in those years is the fact that until 1305 the Masters of the Sacred Palace were all Franciscans, and that two among them were authentic champions of Augustinianism, John Peckam and Matthew of Acquasparta.

It cannot be denied that the exaggerated Aristotelianism of the Averroists proved to be extremely harmful to the moderate Aristotelianism of St. Thomas. But this cannot be considered as the only reason for the condemnations in the year 1277, whereby certain Thomistic doctrines were proscribed along with the Averroistic theses. Properly to understand such condemnations, the general situation of the time must be considered. The condemnations in question were by no means the result of a rash decision on the part of the bishop of Paris, Stephen Tempier, or of the archbishop of Canterbury, Robert Kilwardby. They were rather in accord with the common, if not unanimous, thought of the time. The mere fact that these condemnations have been criticized is not sufficient reason for accepting the thesis of those historians who like to present opposition to Thomism as an act of insolence on the part of certain authoritarian and fanatical masters.

Was not the work of St. Albert the Great and St. Thomas a kind of philosophical revolution? Why, then, should we be surprised if it was not accepted at once by the majority of the scholars? History teaches us that all innovations have a hard time breaking through a well-established tradition. Besides, is it not a significant fact that the dominant figure at the University of Paris in those years was Henry of Ghent, a restorer of traditional Augustinianism?

These considerations, which could doubtless be developed at much greater length, may well serve to throw light on the historical meaning of the so-called anti-Thomism of John Duns Scotus. On the one hand, this anti-Thomism has earned for Scotus the praise of many modern historians, who are far from accepting Thomism as a perfect synthesis. On the other hand, it has been a source of scandal to more than a few Catholic writers, who seem unable to explain it except by an alleged rivalry between Orders and an unrestrained critical attitude. If we bear in mind that during the period of time we have been describing the Subtle Doctor received his education within the Franciscan Order, at Oxford more than at Paris, we should not be suprised to find profound and extensive disagreement between his thought and that of the Angelic Doctor.

Once the existence of the historical contrast between Augustinianism and Thomistic Aristotelianism is admitted, and once this contrast is recognized as being based upon real theoretical difficulties, Duns Scotus' attitude will appear to be a very logical one. If he had not been the hardy thinker he is commonly known to have been, he would have been satisfied, like many other Franciscan masters, with a faithful imitation of the Bonaventurian school. In this case he would not have gone much further than his own masters. He would have been only another Augustinian added to the series of St. Bonaventure's disciples, and his originality would not have amounted to anything worthwhile. For obvious reasons, it is less likely that he would have become a follower of St. Thomas. At any rate, in either case he would have shut himself within the limited horizons of one or the other school.

Things turned out quite differently for him. Powerful thinker that he was, he attempted to overcome the contrast between Augustinianism and Thomism by harmonizing their doctrines into a superior synthesis that would meet the requirements of both schools. This explains why criticism occupies such an important place in his works. Indeed, once the deficiencies of the two schools had been discovered and pointed out, need was felt for a new personal solution of the various problems at issue. This was only the necessary outcome of the very deficiencies of the unilateral solutions suggested by each of the two schools, and could only be obtained by a critical, even though extensive and often subtle, evaluation of the doctrines in question. Such criticism, however, was not directed against Thomistic doctrines alone but against the Augustinian doctrines as well. These latter, as will be presently shown, were even a better target than the others.

What Scotus attempted was far from being something new. Anyone acquainted with the teaching of medieval philosophers must admit that St. Bonaventure, St. Thomas, and, in general, the great masters of the thirteenth century, had attempted to fuse St. Augustine's teaching with the teaching of Aristotle. Reasons, both historical and doctrinal, prompted them to do so. Among the reasons on the doctrinal level, the undeniable fact of the complementary character of the Platonic and Aristotelian, or, as one would say today, the rationalistic and the empirical, points of view, is most important. Yet the approach was not always the same. While in St. Bonaventure it is Platonic Augustinianism that attempts to assimilate Aristotle, in St. Thomas it is Aristotelianism that tries to assimilate Augustine. Indeed, in every philosophical synthesis we have a movement that starts from one of the two points of view just mentioned, and then goes toward the other in order to arrive at a fusion with it. The greater and more logical is the fusion, the deeper and more consistent is the synthesis. It cannot be otherwise. For man does not possess a synthesis; he must struggle to attain it.

Not even Duns Scotus could escape from the law of human imperfection involved in any synthesis of the kind. Therefore, his synthesis is a new attempt to assimilate Thomistic Aristotelianism, which had meanwhile become better known and so better understood and appreciated, into an Augustinianism that, under the pressing criticism of the new Aristotelianism, had become more rigoristic in its essential features. Such being the case, one will readily understand why the Subtle Doctor was preoccupied with disentangling the essential points of Augustinian inspiration from its useless, or at least unnecessary, superstructures. These, he must have thought, had the inevitable effect of weakening its strength and diminishing its appeal.

It has been pointed out that the target of Scotus' criticism is not so much St. Thomas' theories as those of Henry of Ghent. This is true. However, Henry of Ghent, as Gilson well remarks, is for Scotus not so much an adversary to compete with as he is a companion with whom he discusses problems in order to clarify and strengthen a common doctrine. He disagrees with him only on certain particular points, not on the substance of his teaching. Such an attitude can be easily understood in the light of what was stated above: the accurate and continuous criticism that the Subtle Doctor makes of Henry of Ghent's Augustinian theories is due to his preoccupation with presenting Augustinianism in its essential traits, so as to make it a stronger and less rigid system in regard to Aristotelianism. On the other hand, the friendly but constructive character of his criticism finds its explanation in the fact that he himself moves within the same Platonic-Augustinian line of thought, from which he does not depart unless forced to do so.

The difficulty met with in the study of Scotus' thought is also partially due to the fact that such a study presupposes a thorough knowledge of all the thirteenth-century philosophical trends, which the Scotistic synthesis attempts to present in a final critical report. Thus the lacunae in our knowledge of the history of that great speculative century are also the lacunae in our knowledge of the Scotistic thought.

It is the writer's hope that the following pages, which are a summary exposition of the Subtle Doctor's thought, will confirm the truth of his historical hypothesis, namely, that Scotus' philosophy is an Augustinianism that aims to meet Thomistic Aristotelianism, and to fuse it into a more complete and therefore more vital and modern synthesis.

PART TWO
DUNS SCOTUS' THOUGHT

I

THE PROPER OBJECT OF THE HUMAN INTELLECT

TWO DIFFERENT APPROACHES TO PHILOSOPHY

IN PHILOSOPHY more than in any other science the mind of
man reaches the full measure of its ability. Philosophy seeks
to embrace all reality, whereas other sciences study the real
from some particular point of view and within a limited field.
In his inquiry the philosopher may follow either of two ways.
He may start from external reality, as it presents itself to his
experience, and try to discover its laws, causes, and inner unity.
In this case, he begins directly to build up a metaphysics. The
validity of this system and the legitimacy of its conclusions
will be determined by the solidity of its argumentation. However, one may also arrive at metaphysics by way of epistemology,
in which case he starts his speculation with an inquiry about
the human intellect. One may begin, for example, by asking
such questions as the following. How does man know? What
is the process of knowledge? What are the implications of the
intellective act? Does human knowledge have any limits? What
are these limits?

25

The convenience and advantages of the one or the other approach to philosophy have given rise to a great deal of discussion. In our opinion either way is a good and legitimate starting point for philosophy. Metaphysics leads inevitably to epistemology, and epistemology leads to metaphysics. The history of philosophy is a clear demonstration of this truth. On the one hand, human knowledge is a reality that must be explained; on the other, one cannot avoid asking how reality is revealed to the human mind. Difference in the method of inquiry cannot of itself be prejudicial to the possibility of arriving at the same conclusion. Philosophical problems are circular, one demanding the consideration of another. No matter what problem one faces first, one must necessarily face all the other problems at some time. The eventual divergency in the conclusions is not to be attributed to the method of inquiry but to other reasons, such as the difficulty characteristic of the human intellect to see clearly all the problems in their complexity and interdependence. Hence it is extremely difficult for the human mind to give a well-balanced solution that somehow or other will not prejudice a whole system of philosophy.

One of the differences between Platonism and Aristotelianism is precisely this: Platonism tends to base its philosophical inquiry on internal experience; Aristotelianism prefers to begin it with external experience. The Platonic tendency manifests itself clearly in the philosophic trend called Augustinianism, where the problems of the human spirit occupy first place and are the starting point for speculation. Augustinian metaphysics may thus be called a metaphysics of man, in contrast to the Aristotelian-Thomistic metaphysics, which would be a metaphysics of the universe.

Duns Scotus remains faithful to Augustinianism also in this respect.

DUNS SCOTUS' CONCEPT OF THE
PROPER OBJECT OF THE HUMAN INTELLECT

The problem from which a systematic reconstruction of Scotistic thought must take its start is the problem of the proper object of the human intellect. It is only thus that the natural logical order of the Scotistic system is properly emphasized.

The Subtle Doctor was confronted with two conflicting solutions. Henry of Ghent, who was at the time the most influential representative of the Augustinian school, taught that the first and proper object of the human intellect is God, or the supreme being. This thesis is implicitly contained in every theory of intellectual illumination, such as that prevalent, with very few exceptions, among the Augustinians of the thirteenth century. Henry of Ghent is to be credited with having stated explicitly what had been previously said in a confused manner. The advantages of this doctrine are evident. If God is the proper object of the human intellect, one can readily understand why man should not concentrate upon any created thing, for man is led by an interior logic to fix his attention upon what is eternal, infinite, absolute. This deep interior "drive" might well be called man's divine vocation.

In contrast with the Augustinian solution, stands the Aristotelian-Thomistic doctrine, according to which the proper object of the human intellect is the quiddity of a material thing. This is tantamount to saying that the natural object of our knowledge is the essence abstracted from matter. This opinion seems to be confirmed by our daily experience, which shows that all human knowledge has sensation as its necessary starting point.

Duns Scotus is not satisfied with either of the two solutions, and he makes this clear by pointing out their grave disadvantages. When the first object of the intellect is discussed, it is immediately necessary to define the meaning of the term "first." The question, "What is the first object of the human intellect?"

can be understood in different ways. One way of stating it is, "What is the first thing that man knows in the order of time?" Another way is, "What is the most perfect thing (first in the order of perfection) that can be known by the human mind?" Still another way of stating it is, "What is the object to which the human intellect is directed by its very nature?" It is in this third sense that the question is taken here. To ask, therefore, what the first object of the human intellect is, is equivalent to asking, "What is the adequate object, that is, the object that fully corresponds to the natural power of the human intellect?"

Man is not born perfect. This means that man is not in possession from the first moment of his existence of all the acts of which he is capable. Like all other creatures, man is a complex of potentialities, to be developed gradually as he comes in contact with reality. To the law of this gradual development and becoming, not only his body is subject but also his soul. Thus man's intelligence and will have a natural tendency toward the possession of their objects. When this possession is completed, the perfection of these two faculties is attained, i.e., fully actuated.

The object specifies the faculty, i.e., the object is the measure of the perfection of the faculty. Moreover, any development of the faculty is only possible in virtue of its object, in the sense that it is necessarily a pursuit of its object, since it is only in view of its object that the faculty is determined to act.

By applying these general considerations to the particular case of human knowledge, it becomes evident: (1) that the human intellect can know nothing that does not somehow enter the sphere of the natural object for which it was made; (2) that the human intellect knows things in the light of its object, which thus becomes the necessary point of view from which it sees everything. This can be realized in a perfect way, as in the case of God, who knows all possible things in the unique object of His divine mind, or imperfectly, as in the case of man, who does not know all things in the idea of being, yet cannot know anything apart from the idea of being. In fact, "the adequacy of the object," writes Scotus, "can be considered from the point of view of its power *(secundum virtutem)* and from the point of view of its predication *(secundum praedicationem)*. From the point of view of its power, that object is adequate to its faculty which, once it is known, makes all other possible objects knowable to the intellect. In this sense the divine essence is the adequate object of God's intellect. From the point of view of its predication, that object is adequate to its faculty which is *per se* and essentially the predicate of all things that can be known by the intellect."[1]

The following example will help clarify the point at issue. The human eye sees things insofar as they are colored. Even black, which is absence of color, is seen by the eye, but only in opposition or contrast to some other color. If everything were black, the eye would not see anything; it would not see at all. Since reality is seen by the human eye only through color, color is the necessary condition for things to be present to the eye. What has no color is *ipso facto* invisible. Hence color is the primary and adequate object of our power of vision.

There is a perfect analogy between our vision on the sensory level and the vision of our intellect. The proper object of my intellect, then, will be that the presence of which is necessary for seeing things intellectually, and is even the precise reason for seeing them.

CRITICISM OF OPPOSING VIEWS

Having determined the concept of the primary object of the human intellect, it will not be difficult to follow Duns Scotus in his criticism of Henry of Ghent and St. Thomas Aquinas.

God is not and cannot be the primary object of the human

---

[1] *De Anima,* q. 21, n. 2.

intellect. First, because the divine essence cannot be the primary object of my intellect from the standpoint of its predication *(adaequatione secundum praedicationem)*. God would have to be contained within my intellect and be essentially predicable of all the things I know. He would be their common predicate. This is evidently false, since pantheism is false and contrary to our common experience. I can in effect form a perfect concept of man, plant, and the like, without thinking of God, whose concept is entirely different. Secondly, the divine essence cannot be the primary object of my intellect from the standpoint of its power *(adaequatione secundum virtutem)*. To know all real and possible things in God, man would have to have an immediate, perfect, and intuitive knowledge of the divine essence, and not merely an indirect knowledge of it through a painstaking process of concepts and inferences. For it is evident that God, as He is known in our present state, is for us a goal rather than a starting point. This is a knowledge we attain after we know many other things, and not an idea in which we contemplate the ideas, or from which we derive, by analysis, the concepts of other things.

That God is not and cannot be the primary object of our intellect is also manifest from the fact that intuition of God does not naturally belong to man. The divine essence, because of its infinity, is in itself proportionate and adequate only to an infinite intellect, the only intellect that requires an infinite object precisely to exist as an infinite intellect. It is not inconsistent with the human intellect to know the infinite, but such a knowledge is not required by its nature: it can exist as an intellect, even though it has no immediate and direct knowledge of an infinite object. In short, God is not the primary object of the human intellect, because He does not have one of the requirements the primary object of the intellect must have, namely, that of being the point of view from which we know things and the very reason why things are known to us.

On the other hand, we cannot accept the position of St.

Thomas, that the primary and proper object of the human intellect is the essence of a material thing. A material quiddity does not fulfill another essential requirement of the primary object, namely, that of containing under it all that man knows. According to the Angelic Doctor, the object is proportionate to a faculty in the sense that the nature of the faculty determines the nature of the object. This means that a faculty cannot be actuated except by an object of its own nature, or of a nature that is proportioned to the nature of the faculty. Now, there are three kinds of created cognitive faculties or powers. There is a cognitive power that is tied up with matter in its being and operation: the sense. Its object is necessarily linked with matter: it is the singular material. There is another cognitive power that is independent of matter both in being and in operation, that is, the angelic intellect. An angel, by his nature, will be able to know only immaterial things. Between these two is the human intellect, a power which is substantially united with the body in being (*in essendo*), but independent of material organs in its operations. Its proper object, therefore, will be the essences of material things, but insofar as they are abstracted from matter.

It is not difficult to see how in St. Thomas' system gnoseology is made to fit metaphysics.

In his criticism of this opinion, Duns Scotus, as usual, starts from facts of experience. In his scientific and philosophic endeavors, man is stimulated and guided by a natural desire to know the ultimate causes of things, not only in a confused and obscure manner, but clearly and distinctly. When a desire is natural, Scotus remarks, it must also be in itself efficacious, so that it is never absolutely impossible to satisfy it. If, then, the ultimate cause of things is immaterial, as is really the case, it follows that knowledge of the immaterial is not beyond our capacity.

Furthermore, metaphysics studies being in general and not only material beings, which are the object of physics. This means that the human intellect is not confined to the world of material things. This is so true, that even in his present state man can attain some knowledge of God and the soul. Now these facts cannot be explained by one who maintains that the proper object of the human intellect is the essence of a material thing, since we are here confronted with knowledge of objects that transcend the proper object of the intellect. If our mind is capable of going somehow beyond the limits of material beings, it is clear that the quiddity of a material thing is not the proper object of the human intellect.

From the point of view of Christian philosophy, another observation is in order. If the intellect by its nature, that is, insofar as it is substantially united to the body as a form of it, cannot know anything apart from the essence of material things, it follows that as long as it keeps that nature, it will be impossible for it to know immaterial objects. In such a case, there is only one alternative: either we deny to man as such the capacity to enjoy some day the direct beatific vision of God, or we must admit that in heaven man changes his metaphysical nature. Recourse to the *lumen gloriae* is not a solution. For either the *lumen gloriae* changes the nature of our knowing faculty, and then our conclusion is granted, or it does not change it, and then the *lumen gloriae* will never be such as to confer on our intellect the capacity to know an object that in no way enters the sphere of its proper and natural object. Since both consequences are untenable, so also is the doctrine that logically leads to them.

Duns Scotus avoids these difficulties by affirming that the primary and adequate object of the human intellect is neither immaterial being, God, nor material being, nor the *quidditas rei materialis,* but *being* simply and without any qualification, i.e., being as being *(ens in quantum ens)*. Being can be predicated of everything, and nothing can be known that is not a being. Whatever is, by the very fact that it is, is intelligible. It can be the subject of at least one predicate: it exists. For being has the same limits as the intelligible, and only non-being or nothingness is unintelligible to us and to any other intellect.

THE UNIVOCITY OF THE CONCEPT OF BEING

The obvious consequences that follow from such a standpoint did not escape Duns Scotus. The first of such consequences is the univocity of the concept of being. The proper object of a faculty, in the sense that has just been explained, must be only one, just as the faculty is only one. Therefore, in order that being be the proper object of our intellect, and consequently the point of view from which and the reason why we know God and creatures, immaterial and material beings, it must be predicated univocally, i.e., in the same sense, of all things. It cannot be otherwise, for the simple fact that being is the means by which, and the light through which, all things are known.

In the Augustinian philosophy there remained the difficulty of explaining how, from the concept of God, man could descend to the concept of creatures without passing through the intuition of the divine essence. In the Aristotelian-Thomistic philosophy the difficulty was reversed: a way had to be shown how one could ascend from the concept of creatures to the concept of God. Both Augustinians and Thomists solved the difficulty with the doctrine of analogy: an analogy that goes from God to creatures for the Augustinians, an analogy that goes from creatures to God for the Thomists. With his doctrine of the univocity of the concept of being, and consequently of the other transcendental concepts, Duns Scotus opens a new way to the solution of the problem. He does so very modestly, as the following passage indicates:

"In the second place, it can be said, although not definitely because it is not in accordance with the common opinion, that of God we possess not only concepts which are analogous to those of creatures, that is, entirely different from those had of created things, but also concepts which are univocal to God and creatures." [2]

It is a well-known fact that this famous Scotistic doctrine has given rise to many discussions: How must it be understood? What dangerous implications are in it? What are its advantages? To the reader of this study we can offer only a brief and substantial summary of the controversy.

Let us first see the arguments on which Duns Scotus bases his doctrine. His observations on the need for the human intellect to have its own proper object may be considered to be his first argument. To every power there must correspond an adequate object, for it is only from a union of power and object that acts ensue. These acts are the reason for the very existence of the power of which they constitute the natural and necessary perfection. On the other hand, only being in general, that is, being prior to any specification, has the qualities necessary for a primary and adequate object of the human intellect. Hence, unless we wish to maintain that the human intellect is a power without a proper object, we must admit that the concept of being has a real unity of meaning and predication.

"If the predicate *being* is not recognized as univocal to creatures and God, substance and accident—things that are no doubt intelligible to us—we can no longer speak of a primary object of our intellect, either *secundum virtutem* or *secundum praedicationem*. It is only by admitting the univocity of the

<hr/>

[2] *Opus Oxoniense,* I, d. 3, q. 2, n. 5. [Obviously, in this passage Duns Scotus does not use the term "analogous" in the sense it is used by modern Thomists. When he states that the concepts we possess of God are "entirely different" from the concepts we have of creatures, he simply means that the reality expressed by these concepts is in itself essentially different. God is an infinite, self-subsistent being; creatures are limited, participated beings. *(Tr.)*]

concept of being that the proper object of our intellect can somehow be defined." [3]

A second argument is derived by Duns Scotus from the common way of thinking and talking among men. One can doubt whether a thing is God, a supreme and absolute being, or a creature, a relative being; whether it is substance or accident; but one thing is certain, that God, creatures, and accidents are beings. Now a concept or predicate cannot be certain and doubtful at one and the same time and in the same respect. Consequently, if on the one hand I am sure that something is a being, and on the other hand I am not sure whether it is an absolute being (God), or a being that exists *per se* (substance), or a being that exists only in another (accident), it follows that the concept of being is simply different from any one of these concepts and cannot be identified with any one of them although it is included in them all. Therefore, one should admit that the concept of being as such has in itself a unity and consistency that are prior to any further determination. It is a predicate that can be affirmed of all reality in exactly the same sense, i.e., univocally.

Furthermore, we arrive at the concept of God solely through

---

[3] *Ibid.,* q. 3, n. 6. Duns Scotus says *"aliquo modo"* defined, because the concept of *being* is not predicable *in quid,* i.e., essentially, of the transcendentals *unum, verum, bonum,* even though it contains these concepts virtually. These are concepts that cannot be reduced to the concept of being, and therefore are not included in that concept by a community of predication *(propter communitatem praedicationis),* as all other concepts are. They can be reduced to the concept of being in another way, namely, insofar as the concept of being has the power to contain them or contains them virtually *(propter virtualitatem).* For this reason Duns Scotus says *"aliquo modo."* *Being* would perfectly fulfill the conditions of a primary object if it were predicated essentially of all things without exception, or if from the concept of *being* it were possible to derive the concepts of all things, just as the transcendental concepts are derived, or as the divine intellect sees in Its own Essence all other essences.

the study and knowledge of creatures, the only objects that directly move our intellect. How, then, will it be possible for us to obtain from creatures any concept of God, if the ideas we abstract from them are all proper only to created things? If my philosophical inquiry into created reality affords me not only the possibility of forming a concept of God, but compels me to think of Him, this means that, in addition to their proper concepts, creatures suggest to me a concept which does not find its full application in them. In other words, it is a concept that does not belong to them exclusively, and it compels me to admit in addition to them a reality to which the concept itself is perfectly adequate. This concept which I abstract from created beings, but which does not belong to them exclusively, is precisely the concept of being in its most simple signification, and on this I can build my concept of God. Obviously, this would not be possible if the concept of being were not univocal, i.e., common to both God and creatures.

In practice, then, anyone who speaks about God and His perfections admits univocity, even though he may deny it in theory. "Masters, too, when dealing with God and what is known about God, express themselves in such way as actually to admit univocity, even though they deny it in their word." [4]

If the concept of God were from every point of view merely analogous to the concepts we abstract from creatures, we would have to admit that we derive from things a concept much more perfect than themselves. But this is impossible, since no being can of itself give rise to knowledge that is more perfect than itself. Moreover, the strength of all our reasoning, including reasoning about God, rests on the evidence of the first principles. The first principles in turn stem from the concept of being taken in its most simple meaning. How, then, can the

---

[4] *Reportata Parisiensia,* I, d. 3, q. 1, n. 7.

first principles be equally valid for God and creatures, if the concept of being from which they stem is not predicated univocally of God and creatures? Only the univocity of their source guarantees their universal validity.[5]

Nor does it seem possible to save the transcendental character of being, if the univocal unity of its concept in regard to all knowable things is not admitted.

We may ask: Does not univocity endanger the metaphysical transcendence of God, which demands a perfect *otherness* of the divine being in relation to created being? Duns Scotus acknowledges such otherness and affirms it in clear terms: "God and creature are not simply and totally different in their concepts; however, they are simply different in reality, because they have nothing in common on the metaphysical level."[6]

But we may insist: How is a conceptual "community" possible without a real community? Duns Scotus explains this apparent contradiction by pointing out how being is contracted to its inferiors, "uncreated being" and "created being." This contraction is entirely different from the metaphysical process of Porphyry's tree whereby one descends from genera to species. In the Porphyrian tree all transitions are characterized by an increase of reality, inasmuch as in every contraction a further act or perfection is added to the preceding genus. This is not

---

[5] *De Anima,* q. 21, n. 10.

[6] *Op. Oxon.,* I, d. 8, q. 3, n. 11. [Here is Gilson's pertinent observation: "Thus the Scotist univocity is a radical negation of pantheism, since the common attribution of the concept of being to God and creatures requires precisely that it should not be extended to that which makes the being of God to be God; but at the same time it unifies the whole order of human knowledge in affirming the essential unity of its object throughout all the diversity of the states through which it may pass." Etienne Gilson, *The Spirit of Mediaeval Philosophy,* trans. A. H. C. Downes (New York: Charles Scribner's Sons, 1940), p. 266. *(Tr.)*]

true of being, which does not become uncreated or created because of a new added quality specifying it: outside of being there is nothing. In other words, there is no real starting point common to both infinite being and finite being, as there is, for example, for man and horse, who share in common a metaphysical reality, i.e., animality. Infinity and finiteness are not qualities that determine being as by a specific difference, but different intrinsic modes affecting being in its totality. Hence, from the metaphysical point of view, infinite being is totally and absolutely distinct from finite being. Briefly, being is not a genus in reference to God and creatures; nor can it be, because of the essential indetermination of its concept in regard to all things. It is precisely on this indetermination that its transcendentality rests.

Yet, despite the fact that infinite being and finite being are totally different, each of them is a being, i.e., something that really exists. The fact of their real existence is the metaphysical foundation for that conceptual community which is grasped and expressed by the univocal concept of being. No doubt, an intellect capable of knowing all things intuitively would not have to distinguish between being and its intrinsic mode; it would grasp every being in its concreteness as well as in its metaphysical integrity. Such an intellect would not have to be helped by univocal concepts in its knowledge of God, and it could not stop at univocity. But man, who knows only by abstraction and is compelled, as it were, to break up reality in order to assimilate it intellectually, here, too, uses his abstractive power. While in the first moment he grasps only the being of a concrete reality as such, in the second he sees also its mode of being and expresses it by means of a concept that is different from the simple concept of being. Hence univocity is imposed upon us by our process of knowing reality rather than by reality itself. It is a moment in our abstractive process, which is as good and valid as any other kind of abstraction, an imperfect but not a false way of knowing reality.[7]

THE OBJECT OF OUR INTELLECT IN ITS PRESENT STATE

A philosopher like Duns Scotus, who defends the thesis that the proper and adequate object of the human intellect is being *qua* being, must face another difficulty. If our intellect is truly made to know being without any limitation, it seems natural to say that the richer in being a thing is, and consequently the richer it is in perfections, the easier it is for us to grasp it. Thus God, who is being in the most eminent way, should be best known to us, and that almost by a spontaneous, extremely pleasant act. Yet our ideas of God and immaterial beings in general are obtained only with great pain, and even after long meditations they still remain uncertain, confused and vague. On the contrary, our knowledge of material things

---

[7] These thoughts are found in an authentic passage which has not yet been given the consideration it deserves: *Op. Oxon.*, I, d. 8, q. 3, nn. 27 and 29. [The better to explain this somewhat difficult, yet profound doctrine, Duns Scotus makes use of the following example. Suppose there is a whiteness to the tenth degree of intensity. I could conceive whiteness with its degree of intensity, in which case my concept of it would be perfect, for it would give me its full reality. But I could also conceive whiteness while prescinding from its degree of intensity, in which case my concept would only be imperfect, for it would not give me the full reality. This imperfect concept may be common to that particular whiteness and to others, but the perfect concept, i.e., the one including also the degree of intensity, is proper to that particular reality alone. Hence there must be a distinction between that from which a common concept is derived and that from which a proper concept is derived. Such a distinction is not a distinction like that between one reality and another, but like that between a reality and its proper and intrinsic mode. It is in this way that being and its modes are to be understood. *Ibid.*, n. 27. *(Tr.)*]

is much easier and much more perfect. Is not this fact enough
to support the opinion of those who claim that the essence of
material things is the proper object of the human intellect?

Duns Scotus concedes that the intuitive knowledge of being
belongs to man by right. Hence the more perfect a thing is,
the easier, the more pleasant, and the more perfect should be
its union with our intellect. However, this is not the case, because of the conditions in which the human intellect finds
itself at present. "In his wisdom, God has decreed that in its
present state our intellect should understand only those things
whose image is reflected in the phantasm. This is either in
punishment for original sin or because of the natural harmony
existing among the soul's powers in their operations. Thus we
see that the superior power concerns itself with the same object as the inferior power, provided both powers act in a perfect
manner. In fact, it so happens to us that the act by which
the mind thinks the universal is always accompanied by an
act of our imagination. However, this present harmony of
our faculties does not arise from the nature of the human intellect, either because it is an intellect or because it is a human
intellect, that is, an intellect united to the body. If this were
so, then such a harmony should exist even in the glorified
body, which is false." [8]

Two things are certain: first, that, for the reasons just stated,
man's intellect is not by its very nature enclosed within the
limited horizon of material beings; secondly, that in our present state all human knowledge begins necessarily with sensible
things, for they alone are such that they can move and interest
directly our intellective power. Yet it is an undeniable fact
of experience that we can also rise to a certain knowledge of
God and immaterial beings, just as it is undeniable that the
natural way of knowing is by abstraction, that is, a process
whereby we form our concepts in cooperation with sensible

---

[8] *Op. Oxon.*, I, d. 3, q. 3, n. 24.

experience and take our start from material things. Any philosopher wishing to give a complete explanation of human knowledge must take into account these two facts. Consequently, a theory will be judged valid and acceptable only on condition that it furnish a reasonable explanation of these two facts.

The Thomistic theory fails to meet these requirements, not because it affirms that man knows only abstractively, but because it vainly claims to find the cause of this fact in the metaphysical nature of the human intellect. Such an explanation is highly effective as far as the abstractive character of our cognitions is concerned, but it makes any other kind of human knowledge impossible. It forces man inexorably within the limits of sensible experience, more or less as Kant does when he teaches that "pure reason" is barred from the knowledge of what does not enter the a priori intuitions of space and time.

It is precisely to account for the fact that man can rise to some sort of knowledge of God and of immaterial beings, and retain at the same time the possibility of knowing things in a different manner, that Duns Scotus has recourse to his theory of the proper object of the human intellect. This theory must be further explained in the following section.

IMPLICATIONS OF THE SCOTISTIC THEORY OF THE PROPER OBJECT OF THE HUMAN INTELLECT

By its nature (*ex natura potentiae*) our intellect is ordained to know being, being in an absolute sense and without limitations. However, what moves the intellect to know in its present condition is only the quiddity of sensible things, that is, of things which present themselves to our sensible experience. Accordingly, these things are the proper object of our intellect *in movendo* or *in ratione motivi*. If someone were to ask why the human intellect must always act in a way that is inferior to its capacity, he must be reminded of the inscrutable dispositions of the divine wisdom, even more than of the consequences of original sin.[9]

This solution permits Duns Scotus to give an account of both the facts he was called upon to explain. The *ens in quantum ens* as the proper object of the human intellect *ex natura potentiae*—in this respect the human intellect has the same field of vision as any other intellect, for on the one hand, being is by its nature intelligible *(ens et verum convertuntur),* and on the other hand, the intellect is essentially and by its very constitution made to know being which is thus revealed to it—makes it clear that man, even though submerged in the sea of sensible, changeable, and contingent beings, cannot rest and be satisfied with it. He is spurred on by an inner stimulus to overcome it and move upward to the knowledge of God with all the means at his disposal and with a perseverance that defies time and error. Likewise, the fact that the proper object of our intellect *in movendo* or *in ratione motivi* is the quiddity of a sensible thing explains the *manner* in which man knows, that is to say, the need and importance of the abstractive process. This latter is in turn responsible for all the imperfections of human knowledge, since it is only with great

---

[9] This appeal to divine wisdom will no doubt displease the modern mind. However, it is worth noting that Duns Scotus wishes to answer a question that, as a philosopher, he could refuse to answer. After proving, on the one hand, that the human intellect is not enclosed within the limits of material things, and noting, on the other hand, that in its present state it always has to take its lead fron sensible things and work out abstract concepts, he could simply answer anyone asking the reason for such a contrast thus: It is so, because man is made that way. In other words, the mystery lies within man himself; it is not a flaw in Duns Scotus' theory. The answer belongs to theology rather than to philosophy. Hence Duns Scotus would agree with Pascal's statement—already substantially contained in St. Bonaventure and St. Augustine—that only the Christian doctrine can explain the mystery of man.

pain and not without uncertainty that we arrive at an indirect and general notion of God and immaterial beings.

It may not be without interest to point out to the reader, if he has failed to see it himself, that in the first part of his solution—that the proper object of the human intellect considered from the standpoint of its nature is being *qua* being—the Subtle Doctor answers the main difficulty that led the Augustinian school to the doctrine of intellectual illumination, namely, the impossibility on the part of empiricism and the Aristotelian doctrine of abstraction to account for man's knowledge of God and spiritual beings. That this difficulty is the fundamental reason for the Augustinian theory of intellectual illumination has been sufficiently proved elsewhere where the suggestion is also made that such a theory implies a virtual innatism of the idea of God.[10]

Although Duns Scotus accepts the basic requirement for the doctrine of illumination, and in this he is faithful to the speculative tradition of his Order, when he actually faces the doctrine, he refuses to accept it. Furthermore, he rejects the logical consequence of the doctrine of illumination, namely, that God is the first known object of the human intellect. Does he also escape from every sort of virtual innatism? It does not seem so.

It must be recognized that on this point Duns Scotus is far

---

[10] See chap. V of my work, *S. Bonaventura* (Brescia: La Scuola, 1944), and especially my article, "La dottrina bonaventuriana dell'illuminazione intellettuale," in *Rivista di Filosofia Neoscolastica,* XXXVI (1944), 139-58. [The author reaffirms his conviction of the existence of a "virtual innatism" of the idea of God in St. Bonaventure's doctrine in his later work, *Il Problema della conoscibilità di Dio nella scuola francescana* (Padua: Cedam, 1950), pp. 214-42. Other interpreters would limit St. Bonaventure's "innatism" to an *innate facility* man has to attain the idea of God. Cf. P. F. Zacharias Van de Woestyne, O.F.M., *Cursus Philosophicus* (Malines: Typographia S. Francisci, 1925), II, 705-707. *(Tr.)*]

from being clear and explicit. To be sure, he states in several places that even the univocal concept of being, which makes it possible for us to attain to God and to some sort of knowledge of Him, is abstracted from sensible things. However, we are of the opinion that we should cling not so much to the letter of the text as to the logical coherence of the doctrine. Being compelled to start from material being, man cannot form any concept prior to sensible experience. Accordingly, even the concept of being is obtained from sensible experience, and is to that extent an abstract concept. Nevertheless, one should not forget that our concept of being transcends sense knowledge, for the simple reason that the primary and adequate object of the human intellect is being *qua* being. From this it follows that our concept of being, even though it is obtained from sense experience, must be broader than the quiddity of material things. Therefore, it can be rightly affirmed that our intellect, insofar as it is made to know being in its totality, has already within itself, so to speak, a concept of being—*esse,* or "to be"—which makes it possible for man to understand that material reality is not the whole reality, nay, that it is the most imperfect reality.

In such a case, if man arrives at the knowledge of God and is compelled to admit the existence of the absolute, it is not because of what he sees in things, but because of the innate tendency of his intellect to know not just one particular being, but being without qualification, or a being such that its nature transcends the limits of mere sensible knowledge. Thus we are not only allowed to speak of a certain innatism of the idea of being but, in the philosophy of Duns Scotus, we must do so. This type of innatism may be best described as "virtual innatism."

Nor should one forget Duns Scotus' pertinent statement that in distinct knowledge the concept of being is necessarily the first, so that no distinct knowledge is possible except through the concept of being.[11] Once this is granted, the concept of being becomes the necessary requisite and the general condition for all knowledge. This type of innatism shows clearly the extent to which the Augustinian speculative inheritance is still alive in Duns Scotus' thought.*

That the innatism in question refers to the idea of being in general and not to the idea of God—this latter being tied up with the complex structure of the intellectual illumination —is clear from the steps Duns Scotus takes toward Aristotelian naturalism, a system better disposed to accept a solution of the problem of knowledge that is more simple, easier to grasp, and closer to the earthly conditions of man.

In Scotus' doctrine, man's capacity to know God, or better, the need and craving for the divine so much emphasized by the Augustinian school, is given full credit. If our intellect is made to know being, all being, it is evident that by its nature it should be ready and capable for every ascent. Such a destination is the profound, inescapable call with which God draws man to Himself, and with man, all created reality.

---

[11] *Lectura Prima,* I. 17; Vindobonae, Bibl. Nat., Cod. Lat. 1449, f. 18 rb.: "In order to know a thing distinctly, it is necessary first to know being, for being enters into every concept."

* The "virtual innatism" of the idea of being—not of God—which the author attributes to Duns Scotus (a point that he defends extensively in his other work, *Il Problema della conoscibilità di Dio nella scuola francescana, op. cit.,* pp. 348-55, where he states, however, that his is an interpretation "beyond Duns Scotus' statements," *ibid.,* pp. 348-49) has not met with the general approval of scholars. Timothy Barth, O.F.M., in his article "De univocationis entis scotisticae intentione principali necnon valore critico," *Antonianum,* XXVIII (1953), 72-110, substitutes the author's "virtual innatism" with "dynamic innatism," which he explains along the lines of Van de Woestyne (*Cursus Philosophicus, op. cit.,* 2d ed., vol. I, p. 143) as meaning an innate habit or tendency to form without difficulty universal concepts, and especially the transcendental concepts. *(Tr.)*

The preoccupation of guaranteeing man's capacity to arrive at God inspires the Scotistic theory of the proper object of the human mind, just as it inspired all the theories of intellectual illumination worked out by the thirteenth-century Augustinians. This theory, strictly linked up to the doctrine of univocity, is, in my opinion, Duns Scotus' most significant doctrine. It is this, first, because in it we see the solution of the controversy between the Augustinian and Aristotelian schools, which is the scope of all his philosophic endeavors; secondly, because this doctrine offers the key to a full understanding of the Scotistic synthesis both in its spirit and in its intellectual achievement.

II

FINITE BEING

THE VAST field of reality, the whole of reality, lies open before the mind of man. From the first steps of his journey toward being, man is guided by an ideal which moves and directs him, so as to prevent him from stopping short of attaining his goal and fulfilling his natural vocation. This vocation consists in knowing, and therefore loving, not just one particular thing or being, but being in its totality.

The first things that confront man are finite beings, that is, nature in the complexity and variety of its aspects and laws. The philosopher, however, does not restrict himself to a study of things in their material structure; he extends his inquiry to the most universal and most profound aspects of things. Now, the most universal aspect of the beings that constitute the object of our experience is their change and becoming. All things change; in their own way, all things are born, grow, decline, and die. How is becoming possible? Beyond question, this is one of the first problems of philosophy, and it is not without reason that Greek philosophy was born as a philosophy of becoming.

Duns Scotus, like all scholastics, agrees substantially with the Aristotelian solution of the problem of becoming, which rests on the dualistic theory of act and potency (general theory),

47

matter and form (substantial change), and substance and accident (accidental change). Yet he ascribes to Aristotle doctrines that are slightly different from the doctrines attributed to him by St. Thomas. These differences concern mainly the concept of primary matter.

MATTER AND FORM

For both St. Thomas and Duns Scotus, all material beings are composed of matter and form. Matter is the potential element and the principle of indetermination; form is the actual element, as well as the principle of determination. The two doctors also agree in saying that matter and form are two distinct realities, so that their composition is the synthesis of two really distinct principles. But here agreement ends and divergency of opinion starts. Although for St. Thomas matter is something real and distinct from form, it is pure potentiality, having no act of its own. Its act is the form, which, by specifying and determining it, also makes it exist as matter. Accordingly, matter cannot exist without form. It is absurd to say that it can, since it cannot even be conceived as an idea. It exists and is known only through the form, to which it is linked by a transcendental relationship. In this theory both the reality of the composition and the rigorous unity of the composite are saved. The composite is not the result of two things, but of two distinct principles of one and the same thing.

Duns Scotus' departure from St. Thomas' theory is based on his conviction that "it is contradictory to affirm that anything has a purely potential being and that it exists in act." [12] In other words, it is inconceivable for him that a thing should have ontological reality without existing in act. Either matter is not a real principle, and then it has no distinct reality from form, or it is a real principle, and then it must have a reality

---

[12] *Op. Oxon.*, II, d. 12, q. 2, n. 2.

independent of the form. A thing is said to be real when it exists outside its cause, or has the act of existence. Hence, if matter is something real, it cannot be such except through the act that makes it to be matter by bestowing upon it the reality of matter. Even St. Thomas grants that matter is created; it must therefore be something that exists in act. What else is creation but the communication of the act of existence to what was merely possible?

Matter is not *in potentia obiectiva* but *in potentia subiectiva*. To affirm that a thing is *in potentia obiectiva* is tantamount to saying that in reality it is nothing, but that a cause exists which can bring it into existence. On the contrary, a thing is *in potentia subiectiva* insofar as it has the capacity to receive an act or perfection. Evidently, nothing can be *in potentia subiectiva* unless it already exists and is about to receive a further perfection. The consequences of this doctrine are obvious, and Duns Scotus was fully aware of them. They may be summarized as follows:

1. Matter cannot be said to be pure potentiality, in the sense that it has no act of its own.
2. Matter is endowed with an act, the act of being matter, independently of form. Hence it is not absurd to conceive it as existing without form.
3. The composition of matter and form must be understood as a composition of two entities rather than of two principles.
4. Matter is of itself intelligible.

Of these consequences, the third one is by far the most interesting and the most important for tracing the profound meaning of Scotistic thought. It is the concept of the unity of the composite that is here at stake. The most serious charge leveled against Duns Scotus is that by his doctrine he destroys the unity of the composite. In fact, St. Thomas and his school maintain that between two entities no substantial composition is possible. A substantial composition must be between two elements which have a mutual attraction and join together as principles. This means that the reality of the composite has only one act of existence, the act that results from the reciprocal union of the two elements. If the two elements could exist independently of each other, they would be of themselves complete beings or substances: their union would no longer be such as to form just one substance.

Duns Scotus has a somewhat different and, let us say, less rigorous concept of substantial union. For him, to have a substantial union of two elements, it is not necessary that the reality of one element depend on the reality of the other to such an extent that the reality of the two elements is (metaphysically) possible only in the composite. On the contrary, for a real composition, it is required that each element have its own distinct reality, independent as such from the reality of the other. The union does not thereby cease to be a substantial union, provided that the two elements are ordered by nature to constitute one being. This natural determination is enough to assure a metaphysical unity of the composite, as well as being a sufficient criterion for distinguishing a substantial from an accidental unity. An accidental unity is in effect a union of two things that do not manifest a natural determination of one toward the other.[13]

Does this imply, then, that form is not the act of matter? A distinction is necessary. If by act is meant actuality in general, as opposed to pure potentiality, then one must say that matter is *per se* in act without the form. If by act is meant that which gives determination, and by potency that which receives it, then matter is not in act but in potentiality to the form. Inasmuch as matter is capable of receiving all forms— and such is the nature of primary matter—it is only in potency.

---

[13] "Certain things have among themselves a unity of order because they are ordered *ad unum.*" *Op. Oxon.,* II, d. 12, q. 1, n. 14.

As such, it can rightly be called potency to the utmost degree.[14]

The opposite theory runs into a very serious difficulty. If the reality of primary matter depends entirely on the form, it follows that not only matter cannot exist without form in general, but that no matter is possible without a particular form. Whatever exists is necessarily individual. Accordingly, the union that, in the opinion of the defenders of this theory, must necessarily exist between matter and form will certainly not be a mere union between matter and form in general, but between matter and an individual form. This is equivalent to saying that matter can never be separated from the form by which it is actualized here and now—all of which is against their teaching. Hence, if matter is not necessarily united to any particular form, it follows that neither is it necessarily united to form in general. If it can be without this or that form, it can also exist without any form at all. In other words, the bond existing between matter and particular forms cannot be of a different nature from the bond existing between matter and form in general. They are either both contingent or both necessary.

In all this discussion, of which only the fundamental points have been mentioned, Duns Scotus claims to interpret Aristotle's genuine thought. This is so true that to an obvious objection raised against him, namely, that the Stagirite had also denied to God the power to make matter exist without form, the Subtle Doctor answers that this is perfectly understandable in the Aristotelian system. In fact, in the order of nature matter is not separable from form, and the action of the natural efficient causes has no direct bearing upon primary matter. This is

---

[14] *Ibid.,* n. 11: "A being is said to be in potency, inasmuch as the more a thing is lacking in actual determinations, the more it is in potency. Since [primary] matter can receive all substantial and accidental forms, it is in potency to the utmost degree in regard to them. Hence its definition of a being in potency."

possible to God alone. But God, according to Aristotle, never
acts directly upon things, and can not, by reason of His
perfection. He acts solely through the secondary causes. Thus
God's action in the world is limited to the action of the secondary causes. It is only logical, therefore, for Aristotle to deny
to God the power to create matter without form.

It is not within the scope of this study to determine whether
Duns Scotus' interpretation of Aristotle's thought is more
faithful to the Stagirite than that of St. Thomas. The important point for us is to note that the Scotistic conception of
primary matter reflects the fundamental cosmological ideas
of the Augustinian school. For Duns Scotus, as for St. Augustine, matter is the most imperfect being created by God. Nevertheless, as a terminus of the creative act, matter cannot be considered as a purely negative value in the sense that Greek
philosophy considered it. For the Greeks, matter was in effect
something like the principle of evil, the nonbeing of finite
things. In this new conception, the relation between matter
and form is deeply affected, as is the concept of the unity of
the composite. Form loses part of its importance; it is no longer
the act of matter in an absolute sense, for it is reduced to the
precise concept of perfection of matter. The act whereby matter is what it is, on the other hand, is a necessary predisposition
that makes it fit to receive all forms. This is its fundamental
perfection, by which it exists as a receptive capacity for all
further perfections.[15]

This essential characteristic of primary matter renders the
theory of seminal reasons *(rationes seminales)* useless. Inasmuch as matter is by its nature a tendency toward all forms
and a craving for them, it contains them all virtually, and
concurs effectively to their production in cooperation with
the secondary causes. None of the forms that actually determine

---

[15] *Quaestiones subtilissimae in Metaphysicam Aristotelis,* lib. IX, q.
12, n. 2.

matter exhausts the capacity of this latter for further perfection. It is true that one form may prepare matter to receive a more perfect form. However, this is not always the case. When certain matter is determined by a form, its capacity for perfection is restricted, so to speak, within the limits of perfection of the form itself. These limits cannot be overcome by the power of natural agents alone, since these agents meet an invincible resistance in the actual form. Man, for instance, cannot transform a stone into a plant, or a plant into an animal. But none of this is impossible to divine omnipotence.

Just as the act by which matter exists does not prevent matter from receiving the further act of the form, and even makes it capable of receiving it, so the possibility is not excluded that one form may actually enable matter to receive a more perfect form. This latter form will thus be received in virtue of the preceding one. Is not this the doctrine that lies at the bottom of the Augustinian theory of plurality of forms?

THE PROBLEM OF UNIVERSALS

The problem of universals began as a logical problem, but it is also a metaphysical problem whose solution may help considerably to reveal the structure of reality. As usual, Duns Scotus arrives at his own solution of the problem after a thorough discussion of the principal solutions offered by philosophers who preceded him. A new answer would have been useless had the problem already been satisfactorily solved.

Three main solutions of the problem of universals confronted the Subtle Doctor: nominalism, exaggerated realism, and St. Thomas' moderate realism. The Angelic Doctor is never mentioned explicitly by Duns Scotus throughout the discussion, nor does Scotus challenge his position. He rather limits himself to an analysis of the first two systems, nominalism and exaggerated realism, so as to expose their fundamental doctrines and point out their unilateral character and insufficiency.

In any attempt to solve the problem of universals, one is necessarily faced by this evident fact: concrete things are all and always singular, while the knowledge we have of them is in terms of universal concepts. How is this contrast between the singularity of things and the universality of concepts to be explained?

The nominalist answer is that all that exists is *ipso facto* singular, and the universal can in no way be found in the reality of things. The universal must be only in the intellect and from the intellect. If humanity, which is in Socrates, Peter, and other men, were universal, then Socrates, Peter, and all individual men would be universal: in which case universality as such would be destroyed.

Defenders of exaggerated realism answer in their turn: a universal is that which is predicable of a plurality of things. Now, only two alternatives are possible: either this aptitude for predication is to be found really in things, or else it is bestowed upon things by the intellect. If the second alternative is true, it remains to be explained how the intellect confers this aptitude on certain things and not on others, on humanity, for instance, and not on Socrates or Socrateity. On the other hand, when I say that Socrates is a man, or the horse is an animal, my statement has no meaning unless humanity is really in Socrates and animality in the horse. Moreover, if things are only singular, how is it that I know them as universal? Or is my knowledge of them a mere travesty and deformation of reality?

Evidently, nominalism destroys the objectivity of human knowledge. Exaggerated realism on the other hand destroys universality, that is, the predicability of one thing, since all that exists is necessarily this or that and what is proper to every individual.

In Duns Scotus' opinion the solution of this dilemma is possible only through a better understanding and clarification of the concept of universal. On the one hand, the objectivity of our knowledge demands that the universal be somehow in the reality of things; on the other hand, the universal cannot be something real without losing its very nature of universality. This problem can only be solved by considering the complexity and ambiguity of the concept of universal.

By universal may be understood: (1) the relation of predicability between the concept and the things of which it can be predicated; (2) the subject of which it is predicated; or finally, (3) the thing in itself which is predicated.[16] If the term "universal" is taken in the first sense, nominalism is correct, for nominalism considers the universal merely as a product of the mind. If it is taken in the third sense, then exaggerated realism is right. However, both nominalism and exaggerated realism fail to consider the universal in the second sense.

Things are singular, but they are not exclusively such. There are, indeed, certain aspects of things that make them distinct from all other things and so render them unique. There are also aspects that make them really similar to many other things with which they share a unity of genus and species. What makes a thing have a generic or specific communion with others is its common nature *(natura communis)*. Considered in itself, this common nature, e.g., humanity, is neither universal nor singular: it is indifferent to being realized in an infinite number of individuals or in just one individual. While, no doubt, Peter's humanity is not Socrates' humanity, humanity as such *(ex se)* need not be in Peter alone, to the exclusion of all other men. Just as it is not individual by definition, so it need not be in a plurality of individuals. This indifference proper to a common nature may account for this latter's capacity to receive two different modes of being: singularity in concrete things, universality in the intellect. Hence a common nature, i.e., the sum-total of those aspects by which a thing belongs to a species or a genus, is not universal. Nevertheless

---

[16] *Quaest. subt. in Metaph. Arist.,* lib. VII, q. 18, n. 6.

it is the physical basis for the universal—Duns Scotus calls it the *physical universal*—that assures the objectivity of our concepts. When our intellect grasps an object, it concentrates its attention upon the potential indifference of its nature; it points it out, as it were, and actualizes it. The indeterminateness of a common nature is a mere nonrepugnance to being actualized in many things, whereas the indeterminateness of our concept is something positive. This is so true that, while a common nature becomes singular in every individual, its concept refuses to become so. A concept is of its nature universal. It is "indeterminate in act, so that something which is intelligible and numerically one is predicable of every subject and is truly universal." [17]

Thus universality, or indeterminateness in act, belongs only to the concept. It is a modality that things acquire inasmuch as they are known; it is the mode proper to intentional being. However, since it is only in this condition that physical beings enter the metaphysician's domain, Duns Scotus calls the common nature a *metaphysical universal*. This is not a common nature as it is in physical reality, but inasmuch as it is apprehended by the intellect and clad, as it were, in the modalities proper to intentional being.

This still does not give us the universal in its precise formal aspect, namely, in the strict sense of the word. In effect, universality consists in the logical relation whereby a concept can be predicated of many individuals. The study of this particular property of our concepts, with their limits and laws, is the proper object of logic. The logician does not study things directly in their materiality, as the physicist does; nor does he study them in their essence, as the metaphysician would do. He considers only their concepts, or more specifically, things as they are in his mind. Accordingly, Duns Scotus calls the

---

[17] *Ibid.*

concept that is predicable of many individuals a *logical universal*.

To sum up, the universal must have two qualities or properties: it must be in many and be predicated of many *(esse in multis et dici de multis)*. The whole difficulty in the problem of universals is how to reconcile these two apparently contrasting characters. Indeed, what is really in things seems, by this very fact, to be incapable of being predicated *(dici de multis)*, while that which can be predicated *(dici de multis)* seems to be exclusively the product of our intellectual activity.

Duns Scotus solves the difficulty by distinguishing three different meanings of the term *universal:* (1) the universal, inasmuch as it is one in many, is the common nature, which by itself is not apt to be predicated of many— the *physical universal;* (2) the aptitude to be predicated of many which the intellect confers upon common nature in the act of knowing it—the *metaphysical universal;* (3) the actual exercise of this aptitude insofar as the concept, which is in potentiality to be predicated of many, is *de facto* predicated *in actu secundo* by our intellect—the *logical universal*. This last is the result of the act of the intellect which reflects upon the qualities of the concept, and by considering its relation to its subjective parts, discovers that it can be predicated of many individuals.

The physical universal is the real foundation of our concept: it assures the objectivity of our knowledge as well as the real unity of the species and the genus. This unity is called by Duns Scotus a less rigorous unity than the numerical one *(minor unitate numerali)*, because it does not exclude the numerical multiplicity of the individuals. The metaphysical universal, which arises from the thing and the intellect that knows it, represents the necessary link between concrete reality and our logical operations, even though it is formally in the intellect. The logical universal reaps the fruits of that natural collaboration between thing and intellect in which abstraction properly consists. The Scotistic solution of the problem of universals is thus substantially within the frame of moderate realism. The universal is formally in the intellect, but its foundation is in the reality of things.

COMMON NATURE AND THE PRINCIPLE OF INDIVIDUATION

In his endeavor to determine the precise meaning of the foundation of the universal, Duns Scotus elaborated the theory of the *natura communis* or the physical universal. In spite of the many objections that may be raised against the Scotistic *natura communis,* it cannot be denied that this doctrine represents a remarkable step toward greater precision in the terms involved in the problem of universals. It is also a step forward in the proposed solution of moderate realism. Another advantage to be derived from such a doctrine is a better understanding of Scotus' teaching on the metaphysical structure of finite being. If, indeed, the *natura communis* is to be found as such in things, it must have its own reality and metaphysical unity independently of the singularity of things. Duns Scotus accepts such an implication when he states: "The nature by itself is not singular, but is prior to the modality that contracts it to be this or that singular thing; and inasmuch as by itself it is prior to the modality that contracts it, it is not repugnant to it to be without that modality." [18]

This passage, which is only one among the many that could be quoted in support of our assertion, tells us clearly that for Duns Scotus a concrete thing is not merely a composite of matter and form, but also a composite of a specific common nature and of a principle which contracts nature into singularity. By itself *(ex se)* nature, it is worth repeating, is neither universal nor singular. However, as such it does not exist. It exists rather as universal, that is, as an intentional being in the

---

[18] *Op. Oxon.,* II, d. 3, q. 1, n. 7.

intellect, and as singular in concrete reality, outside the intellect. The cause of universality, as will be seen later, is therefore to be found in the intellect, while the cause of the singularity is to be found in something within the thing itself. This is known in history as the problem of, or the quest for, the principle of individuation.

Duns Scotus formulates the problem in these terms: it is not repugnant to the nature or essence of a thing to be participated in by many individuals or to be divisible into many subjective parts. However, once it is actualized in the individual, it loses its divisibility and becomes incommunicable. Incommunicability, or indivisibility into subjective parts, is in fact the characteristic that constitutes the individual.

But what is the cause which brings about that unity which the species acquires in the moment it becomes actualized in the individual? This is precisely the problem at hand. To affirm with Henry of Ghent that individuation does not require a positive principle because the essential characteristics of the individual are negative, i.e., they consist in the intrinsic indivisibility and incommunicability of the individual to other things, is not to solve the problem but to avoid it. For we are trying to find out precisely what is the cause that makes these characteristics proper to the individual and not to the specific essence. Negative as they may be, they must be based on something real, namely, the real modification that explains their appearance. Hence the principle of individuation must be sought in something positive. This is the opinion of Godfrey of Fontaines, Giles of Rome, and St. Thomas Aquinas. Duns Scotus analyzes their solutions and makes his own remarks upon them.

The Thomistic solution, which places the principle of individuation in *materia signata quantitate,* is well known. Godfrey of Fontaines and Giles of Rome agree substantially with St. Thomas; but whereas Aquinas lays emphasis on matter rather than on quantity, they consider quantity rather than matter to be responsible for individuation.* Despite the undeniable differences between the solution of Godfrey of Fontaines and that of Giles of Rome, the Subtle Doctor for practical purposes reduces both solutions to one. His criticism is mainly based on the fact that quantity is an accident. Hence the dilemma: either substance is identical in all individuals, so that the multiplication of the individuals within the same species is effected only through the difference in the quantities that always accompany material beings, or substance is by its nature singular and manifests its singularity by demanding an appropriate quantity from which its multiplication derives. In the first case, there is renewed the Platonic error of a separate and perfect specific essence, with all the consequences that follow from it, the first of which would be to reduce the principle of multiplication of the individuals to the level of an accident. In the second case, something even more absurd is affirmed, namely, that a substance, which by itself is singular, and hence indivisible into subjective parts, is so deeply modified by an accident, i.e., quantity, that it becomes divisible into subjective parts. That an accident may change the nature of a substance is something unheard of. Furthermore, it is contradictory.

The Thomistic doctrine, which makes the principle of individuation and distinction what by its nature is indeterminate and indistinct, is no better a solution than the preceding one.

To avoid these difficulties and save the dignity of the individual, Duns Scotus has recourse to his theory of "haecceity," or thisness. The principal argument on which he bases his solution is this. The species possesses a unity of its own, which

* Godfrey of Fontaines maintains that form is the principle of individuation, not matter or quantity. "Formalis ratio huiusmodi distinctionis, qua scilicet unum individuum in materialibus ab alio formaliter distinguitur . . . est forma substantialis uniuscuiusque individui." *Quodlib.* VII, q. 5, ed. De Wulf-Pelzer-Hoffmans, *Les Philosophes Belges* (Louvain, 1904-35), vol. III, p. 324. *(Tr.)*

is not only a logical unity but also a natural one. It is a unity that, though excluding a division into essential parts—any modification of the essential elements destroys the species—does not exclude a division into subjective parts, whereby the representatives or carriers of the species can be multiplied indefinitely.

The individual possesses a unity that is more perfect than the specific unity, for it excludes even the division into subjective parts. The individual is the only representative of itself. Now unity and entity proceed together: a more perfect unity demands a more perfect being. Hence the transition from specific unity to individual unity cannot take place without the addition of an intrinsic perfection to being itself. This new act, or entitative perfection, that is added to the species is what Scotus calls "haecceity." It is not a new formal element in the sense that the specific difference determines the genus, but an entity "which determines, as by an act, that which may be called a possible and potential reality of the species." [19] In other words, the haecceity is not just a perfection added to the form and within the form, but a new mode of being that affects matter, form, and the composite, i.e., the whole common nature, which is thereby contracted and forced to come out of that sort of indetermination which is proper to the specific nature.[20] It is on the plane of act, and therefore a real principle, without being a formal element. This is not inconsistent with Duns Scotus' philosophy, according to which matter, as previously stated, has an act of its own independent of the form.

The haecceity is not an enrichment of the form in its quidditative being *(in esse quidditativo)* but rather the last step or the ultimate preparation of the form, and therefore of the whole composite, toward and for real existence. "This reality

---

[19] *Op. Oxon.,* II, d. 3, q. 6, n. 12.
[20] *Ibid.,* n. 15.

of the individual [i.e., that which makes something to be individual] can never be understood as a new form but rather as the ultimate reality of the form." [21] This haecceity is totally different from, and has nothing in common with, other haecceities, "because every individual entity is radically different from any other entity." [22] Herein lies the reason for the impredicability of the individual, which can receive all predicates but cannot in turn itself become a predicate.

Looked at from this point of view, the individual substance shares in one characteristic of matter. It can be said that haecceity, logically considered, constitutes the individual in its receptive character *(in ratione subiicibilis),* and consequently in its material being *(in esse materiali).* Indeed, only that which is predicable has the character of form *(habet rationem formae).*[23] This explains why Aristotle never disjoins the individual from the concept of matter.

In short, one should not conceive the composition of common nature and haecceity, which contracts it, as a real composition, analogous to the composition that results from the union of matter and form. Haecceity is not a really distinct principle, but merely the ultimate entity of form, or its ultimate necessary perfection in the order of being. Common nature can never exist without haecceity, nor is it related to it as one thing to another, but as reality to reality, that is, as a mode of being to a mode of being of one and the same thing.[24] Between them there is only a formal distinction.

It is time now to consider the important consequences deriving from the Scotistic doctrine of the principle of individuation. The first of these is a radical vindication of the value of the individual against the depreciating tendencies of Greek

[21] *Ibid.,* n. 12.
[22] *Ibid.*
[23] *Ibid.,* n. 13.
[24] *Ibid.,* n. 16.

philosophy. For Plato the only realities in the full meaning of the term were ideal essences. The multiplicity of individuals was for him a degradation and devaluation from which, quite inconsistently, man alone could redeem himself. Aristotle, too, did not depart on this point from the logical course of Platonic metaphysics. He taught, in fact, that only the form or essence is intelligible, while the individual is the result of a somewhat mysterious contamination of being (form) and nonbeing (matter). Furthermore, through his doctrine of a separate agent intellect, Aristotle, more consistently than Plato, even reduced the individual man to a feeble incarnation of the species. In so doing, he ended up by betraying the metaphysical insight which had marked the starting point of his thought, namely, that things exist only as individuals, and therefore "the individual (and not the species) is being and one in the most true sense."

It is hard to understand how statements of this kind can have a real meaning, unless an entitative perfection superior to the perfection of the specific essence is recognized in the individual. The admission of this further perfection in the individual seems also to be the necessary requirement for salvaging the value of human personality, which is one of the postulates of Christianity. Here is where the true meaning of the Scotistic doctrine of haecceity is to be found. This doctrine aims precisely at pointing out the individual's greater richness of perfection in contrast to the species, and at explaining how things cannot exist except as individuals. Individuality, in Scotus' system, is the ultimate perfection of things: it enables them to receive in themselves the act of existence. Only thus they become *real* in the full sense of the term.

If the individual is a more perfect being than the specific essence, it will not only have a greater unity, but also a greater degree of truth and goodness. The individual will be cognizable in itself. If our intellect does not succeed in penetrating the whole richness of reality enclosed in it, that is exclusively because of its weakness. But God knows it, and to each in-dividual He has assigned a definite place in the harmonious complexity of reality. Each individual is like a note in the grand symphony of creation and furnishes new evidence of God's magnificence and bounty. As Duns Scotus puts it, "In-dividuals as such are also willed by the first cause, not as ends—for God alone is the end—but as something ordered to the end. Hence God multiplied the individuals within the species in order to communicate His goodness and His beatitude." [25]

Finally, let us not forget that Scotus' doctrine of the prin-ciple of individuation is a transcendental doctrine. As such, it embraces all beings and is not limited as is the Thomistic doctrine, to material beings.* Once again the Subtle Doctor appears to be in harmony with the exigencies of the Augustinian school. His theory of haecceity is an attempt to bring forth and give more concrete shape to some of the thoughts under-lying Augustinian doctrines concerning the specific as well

---

[25] *Ibid.,* q. 7, n. 10.

* St. Thomas applies his doctrine of the principle of individuation also to the soul, but only insofar as the soul is related to the body: "anima non individuatur per materiam ex qua sit, sed secundum habi-tudinem ad materiam in qua est." *De Anima,* art. 6, ad 13. Concerning the Thomistic and Scotistic doctrines on the principle of individuation, Hans Meyer writes: "The Thomistic principle of individuation has evoked much criticism, not only because St. Thomas was uncertain about it or because it was improperly understood, but especially because of the inherent weakness of the Thomistic position." *The Philosophy of St. Thomas Aquinas,* trans. Rev. Frederic Eckhoff (St. Louis: Herder Book Co., 1948), p. 76. "When St. Thomas placed the principle of individuation for immaterial things in the form, and for material things in matter, establishing a double explanation, he made known his in-ability to find a uniform basis for the solution. Scotus was disturbed by

as individual multiplicity of the angels and the possibility of knowing the singulars.

ESSENCE AND EXISTENCE

In order to understand the metaphysical structure of finite being, one more step must be taken: we must consider the act of existence. Duns Scotus rejects explicitly the idea that the act of existing may be thought of as the principle of individuation. Haecceity is still on the plane of essence; it constitutes the ultimate perfection of the individual essence. What participates in the notion of essence is not included in the notion of existence. Existence makes a mere possible being to be an actual being; it actualizes essence, but it does not modify it. Its relation to essence is far from being a predicamental relation, for existence is neither substance nor accident, neither nature nor individuality. Existence is related to essence in an entirely different manner.

Are essence and existence in a finite being really distinct from one another? Before giving Scotus' opinion on this point, let us make it clear that the essence in question is not a possible essence, but a real one, and by real essence we mean an essence which is outside of its cause *(extra causam suam)*. Hence the problem may be stated this way: can an essence be real without its act of existence? Duns Scotus does not treat this question specifically; however, certain statements in his works leave no doubt as to his opinion on the matter. "That an essence be outside of its cause and have no reality to make it that par-

---

this deficiency, and, later on, it led the youthful Leibnitz to reject the Thomistic solution." *Ibid.*, p. 77. "Scotus halted the trend of thought fostered by the teachings of Aristotle and St. Thomas which tended to degrade the individual in favor of the universal." *Ibid.*, p. 79. *(Tr.)*

ticular essence *(non habeat aliquod esse quo sit essentia)* is for me a contradiction." [26]

Duns Scotus has often been criticized for not having understood the Aristotelian-Thomistic concept of potency as something deprived of any kind of actuality. To a certain extent this is true. In fact, he was never able to understand how a potency could be said to be real, i.e., outside its cause, and at the same time have no act of its own to constitute it as a real potency, be it primary matter or essence. This apparent lack of understanding is common to the whole Augustinian school. No critic of Scotus, however, has ever thought of asking himself whether such a lack of understanding might not be attributed to the difficulties inherent in the very notion of the Aristotelian potency, especially when such a notion is viewed from the standpoint of the creationist theory. May not Duns Scotus perhaps be right when he says that such a notion involves a contradiction? Whatever the case may be, one thing must be borne in mind: it is precisely in this contrast of views that lies the root of all the differences that distinguish Duns Scotus' metaphysics from the metaphysics of Aristotle.

---

[26] *Op. Oxon.*, II, d. 12, q. 1, n. 16. [That Duns Scotus is opposed to the real distinction between essence and existence in real things is also manifest from the following texts: "Nescio enim istam fictionem, quod *esse* est quid superveniens essentiae." *Op. Oxon.*, IV, d. 11, q. 3, n. 46. "Simpliciter falsum est, quod *esse* sit aliud ab essentia." *Ibid.*, d. 13, q. 1, n. 38. ". . . propositio est falsa: sicut se habet *esse* ad essentiam, ita operari ad potentiam, quia *esse* est idem realiter cum essentia." *Ibid.*, II, d. 16, quaest. unica, n. 10. Hans Meyer seems to agree with Duns Scotus when he states: "The theory of the real distinction maintains that the existing essence of a thing is really distinct from its existence, which is contradictory." *The Philosophy of St. Thomas Aquinas*, p. 96. *(Tr.)*]

III

MAN

THE DIVERGENCE of opinion between St. Thomas and Duns Scotus with regard to the concept of potency has a bearing on the fundamental problem of psychology, the relationship between soul and body. The Scotistic solution is characterized by the theory of the form of corporeity *(forma corporeitatis)*.

THE FORM OF CORPOREITY

It is well known that in the middle ages biology was far from being the highly developed and accurate science that it is at present. Yet medieval scholars understood that life is a very special process that cannot be reduced to matter or explained in terms of physical and chemical laws alone. The source or principle of life is what they called "soul." However, it was felt that for the soul to be present and to act, there was need for matter already prepared by some kind of mixture and organization of the material elements. The basic difference between modern vitalistic biology and medieval biology consists precisely in this, that for us today organic activity is synonymous with life, so that it is impossible to conceive the organization of a living body without the positive action of a vital principle or soul. Moreover, the soul is believed to be present in the very moment of the formation of the first living cell of a being as a vitalistic impulse for all the organic processes. In the middle ages, on the contrary, it was commonly agreed that the soul could not make its appearance until matter was adequately prepared by the action of successive forms. However, this succession of forms was differently conceived by the Augustinian and the Aristotelian-Thomistic schools. Whereas St. Thomas believed that the more perfect form virtually contained within itself the powers of the inferior forms, which would therefore become useless and cease to exist upon the appearance of a superior form, the followers of the Augustinian school maintained that this last form would not destroy the preceding ones but only subordinate their action to its own. Thus for St. Thomas the unity of the human composite was warranted by the unicity of the form, whereas for his opponents the unity of the human composite was sufficiently guaranteed by the natural subordination of the lower forms to a superior and more perfect one.

Duns Scotus does not completely accept either point of view. He agrees with the Thomistic principle that it is useless to admit the presence of a plurality of forms when the more perfect form contains within itself the powers of the inferior ones. At the same time he believes that this principle of metaphysical economy, namely, that beings are not to be multiplied without necessity, cannot be wholly applied to the case of man and living beings in general. Life is something entirely different and must be explained in an entirely different manner. "The form of life is by its nature more noble than any organic form of the compound *(forma mixtionis)*. Hence the principle of life must be more perfect than the principle of organization considered as such. Consequently, even though in the vegetative and animal kingdoms the same subject transmits both corporeal elements and soul, there are in it, as it were, two agents, for it performs two actions, one of which is absolutely more perfect than the other." [27]

A living body is not merely a composite substance like a material being, but a substance that, in addition to being composite, is also endowed with life. There must therefore be two distinct principles, one to explain composition *(forma mixtionis)*, and the other to explain life *(forma vitae)*, for life is a very special fact of a higher order which simply transcends any purely material composition. The distinction between these two principles and the irreducibility of life to a simple composition of elements can be observed at the moment of death. Death, which is the separation of body and soul, the latter being here understood in the general sense of vital principle or *forma vitae,* does not involve immediate destruction of the body as a material compound. The body remains in its physical integrity as a body of that particular living being even after death. What is it, then, that confers on the corpse of a loved one the actuality of being the corpse of a man rather than of a beast, of being the corpse of a certain beloved person rather than of another? What is it that continues to mould, so to speak, the manifold of elements that constitute the dead body and that preserves in it the appearance and the particular features that make it dear to me? It cannot be the soul, answers Duns Scotus, for the soul has already departed from the body; it must therefore be the form of corporeity. This is not just the form of corporeity in general, like that admitted by the older Augustinian school, but a determined, specific, and individual form proper to the body of each living being. It is the kind of form that confers on a certain material compound the actuality of being the body of this or that particular material being.

The form of corporeity is the ultimate disposition of matter that enables it to receive the soul. It is therefore a form prior

---

[27] *Op. Oxon.,* IV, d. 11, q. 3, n. 45.

to the soul to which it is ordered and with which it remains. It is an indispensable perfection that makes a material compound able to be informed by the soul as the *forma vitae*.

If the form of corporeity is the perfection disposing the body to be actually informed by the soul, does it not follow that once the soul or life withdraws from the body, the disposing action of the form of corporeity on the material compound also comes to a standstill? How can the form of corporeity remain without the soul? Does it not cease to exist even before the soul's departure? In answer to this objection Duns Scotus states that the form of the compound *(forma mixtionis)*, precisely because it is by its nature ordered to the soul, acts in a perfect way and with all its power only when it is united to the soul. It thus communicates to the compound and maintains in it the harmony of qualities and proportions necessary for the vegetative, sensitive, and intellective life. When for one reason or another this equilibrium of dispositions in the compound is broken, and the soul, no longer finding the indispensable conditions for its permanence in the body, withdraws from it, or ceases to exist, as is the case with plants and brutes, the form of the compound *(forma mixtionis)* still remains, but it becomes feeble and weak. This explains why the process of dissolution of the compound into its elements, which we call putrefaction, starts almost immediately after death.

DOCTRINE OF PLURALITY OF FORMS

On the basis of the foregoing doctrine, there are in man, as in any other living being, two forms, the form of corporeity and the soul. Moreover, the form of corporeity is ordered and subordinated to the soul. It is not necessary, however, to distinguish between a vegetative, sensitive, and intellective soul, for the intellective soul has within itself the powers of the lower souls. Will not this doctrine endanger the unity of the human composite? Unity follows being, and being is one. It is that specific being precisely because of its form, which must be unique for each thing.

This is the main argument advanced by upholders of the Thomistic theory of unicity of form. Were there several forms, there would also be several acts of being, and therefore several beings.

It is enough to recall what has been said in the preceding chapter in order to know Duns Scotus' answer. In fact, he merely repeats what he has already stated: I cannot conceive how a thing can be real without its act of existence, that is, without existing. If a substance is composed of real parts, it cannot have just one act of being, since each part, in order to be real, must have its own act of being. Hence, the actuality of the compound is consequent upon the actuality of all the parts. "I do not understand why the *esse* which is added to a composite essence cannot be itself composite. Rather, the *esse* of the whole compound includes the *esse* of all the parts, as well as the many partial *esse* of the many parts or forms [by which it is composed], just as a being that contains many forms includes all those partial actualities." [28]

For the unity of the compound it is of course necessary for one form, the last and most perfect one, to control and perfect by its actuality the actuality of the partial forms, so as to keep them together as by a natural bond. If there were no such subordination, and if all the forms of a compound were on the same level of perfection and importance, the unity of the compound would be impossible. But this is not the case.

To sum up, the unity of the compound does not require unicity of form, but only a natural subordination of partial forms to the ultimate and most perfect form, in which the perfection of the being they help to constitute is completed.[29]

---

[28] *Op. Oxon.,* IV, d. 11, q. 3, n. 46.
[29] *Ibid.*

If this is the case, will not all distinction between substantial form and accidental form be ruled out? Substantial form is the form that gives *esse simpliciter* to what was only in potency; accidental form is the form that modifies an already existent thing. It does not give *esse simpliciter,* but only a certain *esse,* an *esse secundum quid* or qualified *esse.* Now, if the theory of subordination of forms in the compound were true, the last perfecting form could not be called a substantial form, for it does not give *esse* to the compound in the simple sense of the term. It merely modifies the *esse* of the parts, inasmuch as it causes it to become a subordinate *esse.*

Duns Scotus answers this objection by further clarifying the meaning of the term *esse simpliciter.* Form does not give *esse simpliciter,* if by that is meant the act of existence whereby a thing exists outside of its cause and emerges from nothingness, as previously stated. Prime matter, for example, exists, that is, it is beyond nothingness, even before it receives any form. Form confers only the formal *esse;* it does not cause a thing to exist *simpliciter,* but only to exist as such, that is, with all its generic, specific, and individual determinations. It is a substantial form when it is actually the root of those essential determinations without which a thing cannot be that thing; it is an accidental form when it confers only such determinations as may or may not be in the thing without this latter ceasing to be what it is, i.e., man, plant, horse, Socrates, etc. Since it is through the substantial form that a thing is what it is *simpliciter,* whereas through the accidental form it exists in a particular modified way, it may be said that substantial form confers *esse simpliciter,* whereas a particular form confers *esse secundum quid.* One should never forget, however, that in this case the *esse simpliciter* is always formal being: it is *esse simpliciter* only in a more restricted sense.

It has been necessary to review these various points of Scotus' answer, for in them we find not only a justification of the form of corporeity, but also the doctrine of plurality of forms in general. Even though Duns Scotus, in conformity with the law of metaphysical economy previously mentioned, applies this doctrine only to living beings, and to man in particular, it is worth pointing out the fact that this Scotistic doctrine is possible only on the basis of general principles common to the Augustinian school. All that Duns Scotus brings to it is greater precision of concepts and formulas.

THE INTELLECTIVE SOUL AS FORM OF MAN

The human soul is spiritual or immaterial. This is not only the common teaching of the best philosophical traditions, but also a doctrine that can be proved by a rigorous rational demonstration. Duns Scotus' attitude toward this problem is characterized by a twofold concern. If, indeed, all philosophers agreed that the principle of intellectual operation must be spiritual, not all of them were of the opinion that this principle must belong formally to man. At the time of Duns Scotus, Averroism had not yet laid down its arms. "That cursed Averroes," to use Scotus' words, "in his fiction of *De Anima*, lib. 3, which is incomprehensible to himself and to others," affirmed precisely "that the intellect is a separate substance that can be united to us through the phantasms." [30] It is not enough, therefore, for Duns Scotus to demonstrate that understanding is a spiritual operation; he must also show that it is an operation proper to man. The two things are equally important.

An a priori study of man's nature is impossible. The only way we can know it is by studying its acts and, by way of causality, arrive at their adequate principles. Accordingly, the theme of the thesis will be expressed in these terms: "Understanding is an operation proper to man; as such, it must come

---

[30] *Op. Oxon.,* IV, d. 43, q. 2, n. 5.

from his form. Since this form is of an intellectual nature, the intellective form is the proper form of man."[31] Demonstration of this thesis tends to establish, first, that man's cognitive activity cannot be reduced entirely to sense knowledge; and second, that if man is capable of spiritual acts and operations, he must have within himself a principle of spiritual activity as his essential perfection.

To prove the first point, it is customary to stress the immaterial character of our knowledge. However, the term "immaterial," remarks Duns Scotus, is not so clear as to make an explanation unnecessary. Immateriality, for example, might be taken merely to mean a particular organ's independence in acting. Strictly speaking, such an immaterial operation does not as yet require a spiritual form. It could very well be the operation not simply of a special organ but of the whole corporeal compound. The term "immaterial" can also be taken to mean inextended. In this sense understanding would have nothing in common with matter.

That human understanding actually possesses this prerogative can be demonstrated, first of all, by the fact that we can reflect upon our own acts, and secondly, by qualities proper to the object of our intellectual knowledge. What is extended is incapable of reflection, since the act of reflection demands a complete and perfect folding back upon itself, and this is incompatible with the presence of quantitative parts. Moreover, man reasons about being in the full extent of the term, and does not limit his considerations to being as it is presented to this or that sense, nor to sense perception in general. He knows the universal as well as the relationships existing between the essences of things. He also knows inferentially things that he does not perceive through his senses. All these forms of cognition are inconceivable in a being whose power does not extend beyond the sensible level. The senses cannot reach beyond

---

[31] *Ibid.*, n. 6.

objects determined here and now in their existential actuality.

That these intellectual acts are truly our own acts is evident from our consciousness of them, the kind of interior intuition that makes us sure of something even though we cannot prove it, simply because it is self-evident. If anyone challenged the truth of the foregoing statement, Duns Scotus would simply say: "Further discussion with such a man is useless and we must tell him that he is a mere animal, just as we would not argue with a man who denies he sees a color present to his senses but would tell him his eyes are sick or he is completely blind." [32]

Therefore, it is man that knows by reflection his own acts; it is man that knows being as being, the universal, the relations among essences; it is man that develops and widens his knowledge by reasoning. Yet these acts are not absolutely identical with his essence. This is so true that we can be men without actually knowing, which means that the proximate subject of these acts is only a part of man. It cannot be an organ, nor can it be the human composite as such, since they are both extended and incapable of inextended acts. It must be something inextended, namely, the intellective soul.

That the relationship between man and the intellective soul is identical with the relationship between a thing and its form is manifest from what has just been said: it is man, in the formal sense of the term, that knows. Were it not so, I could never say, "I know," but would have to say, "It is the soul in me that knows." I would thus go against the interior evidence referred to.[33]

Thus far Duns Scotus has not made any substantial innovation on what is found in the doctrine of St. Thomas. His

---

[32] *Ibid.,* n. 11.

[33] *Ibid.,* n. 12: "The intellective power is inherent in us as a form; otherwise, it could not be said that we understand in the true sense of the term."

originality consists rather in the parallel argument that he derives from the consideration of the acts of our will. The essential characteristic of our volitional acts is their freedom, that is, the power to choose between two opposite things, and to revoke the choice once it has been made. Volitional acts must therefore be rooted in a different form that transcends all sensible forms. Hence the soul, an inextended and immaterial form, reveals itself to us as the principle of intellectual and volitional acts. It is intellect and will.

RELATIONSHIP BETWEEN THE SOUL AND ITS FACULTIES

How must the relationship between the soul and its two faculties and between the two faculties themselves be conceived? Duns Scotus is of course acquainted with the Aristotelian and Augustinian doctrines. St. Thomas teaches that intellect and will are two properties of the soul, and hence that the soul belongs to the category of substance, while its two faculties belong to the category of accidents. This is tantamount to saying that there is a real distinction between the soul and its faculties. St. Thomas' fundamental argument for his thesis is this: potency and act are in the same genus or category. But to know and to will are accidental acts that cannot be identified with the soul, which exists even when it does not think or will. Therefore, the power to know and the power to will are also in the category of accidents.

Duns Scotus takes exception to the major of the syllogism. The term *potentia,* he observes, has two entirely different meanings. There is a potency or power in the order of act or operation, and there is a potency in the order of being. The first is divided into active and passive potency, depending on whether it is an efficient principle or a receiving principle of operation. In this case—namely, when *potentia* is considered in the order of act or operation—the major of the syllogism is false, "because an accident is immediately rooted in the substance, otherwise there would be an infinite regress." [34] Some accidental modifications must inevitably be rooted in the substance without any intermediary factor. If every modification presupposed another modification, a substance could never be modified or be the subject of change or becoming. At least in some cases, therefore, it is necessary that potency or power remain in the same category of substance, while operation belongs in the category of accident.

The major premise of the syllogism is only true when it refers to potency taken in its second meaning, namely, as a constitutive principle, together with its adequate act, of something that is either substance or accident.

As regards their acts, intellect and will are potencies or powers taken in the first sense of the term. Whether they are active or merely passive powers will be shown in the next chapter. Hence there is no metaphysical necessity to force these two powers into the category of accidents simply because their acts belong to the category of accidents.*

The Augustinian opinion, which Duns Scotus, as usual, examines in Henry of Ghent's formulation, maintains that in-

---

[34] *Op. Oxon.*, II, d. 16, q. unica, n. 5.

* Scotus' point is to show that St. Thomas' argument for the real distinction between the soul and its faculties is not valid, or at least it does not apply to the problem at issue. Hence his distinction of *potentia* considered as a power and *potentia* considered in the order of being. The scholastic axiom, potency and act are in the same genus (*actus et potentia sunt eiusdem generis*), is valid for *potentia* considered in the order of being only. When considered as a principle of operation, a power or *potentia* can belong to one genus or category—in our case, the category of substance—and its acts to another genus or category, i.e., the category of accidents. This, however, does not mean that a power must be identified with the substance or nature of the being in which it resides. A distinction is conceivable between substance and power, the soul and its faculties. The exact type of this distinction is the subject of the discussion immediately following. (*Tr.*)

tellect and will are identical with the soul's essence. They are merely different ways by means of which the soul establishes its contact with things. Intellect is the soul insofar as it knows; will is the soul insofar as it wills. Duns Scotus believes that this is no solution of the problem. The problem at issue is not the diversity of the acts, but the intrinsic basis of this diversity as well as the immediate principle of the acts themselves. The immediate principle of different acts cannot be formally identical. There would be no reason or explanation for such a diversity.

Hence intellect and will are not really distinct from the essence of the soul, but at the same time they cannot be identified with it. The first solution, that of St. Thomas, is not based on arguments of metaphysical necessity; the second solution, that of Henry of Ghent, does not solve the problem. Between these two solutions another is possible which holds a middle place and avoids the two extremes: intellect and will are distinct from the essence of the soul, but only *formally*. This is the Scotistic solution.

It is not easy to grasp the meaning and value of the formal distinction met so often in the works of Duns Scotus. Formal distinction stands between real distinction and distinction of pure reason or logical distinction. There is a real distinction between two things, when the one is not contained in the other either as a fruit is contained in the germ, an effect in the cause, or something distinct is contained in something confused: one thing is perfect in itself apart from the other, so that they are two really different things. The logical distinction, on the other hand, is nothing but a distinction of concepts as regards a thing that is really and formally identical. On the contrary, two entities are formally distinct from one another when, although one is not contained in the other in any of the three ways mentioned in connection with the real distinction, i.e., potentially, virtually, or confusedly, they nevertheless lack that ultimate perfection which would make them *really different.* It is only because they are united together that they constitute a real thing. However, they are not parts or constituent principles of the thing, but only different formalities of it.

A typical example of Scotus' formal distinction is found in being and its transcendentals, the one, the true, and the good. Unity, truth, and goodness are not only concepts, but real aspects different from the entity. They are in a concrete being, but are not contained in that entity, as act is in its potency, or as an effect is in its cause, or as something distinct is in something confused. They are attributes that affect the complete entity, but each in its own way, in virtue, as it were, of an innate right. They are different formalities, without being at the same time either substantial or accidental forms of the entity. Being is consequent upon their union; yet they cannot be called either parts of being or its principles, just as their union cannot be called composition. They are mutually related, and one is absolutely nothing without the others; yet none of them receives anything from the others. In the union each one keeps intact its own formality. However, the entity enjoys a primacy that is not only logical but also metaphysical in regard to unity, truth, and goodness which flow from the entity without being accidents of it. The technical term naming this characteristic relationship between being and its transcendentals is *passio:* unity, truth, and goodness are *passiones entis.*[35] "Just as being," says Duns Scotus, "sums up in itself the reasons for its own unity, truth, and goodness, and yet does not thereby confuse them, so the soul unites within itself these powers [intellect and will], even though they are formally distinct."[36]

Formally, the human soul is neither intellect nor will. In turn, intellect is entirely different from will. Yet, without intellect and will a rational soul can neither have a concrete

---

[35] *Ibid.,* n. 17.
[36] *Ibid.*

existence nor can it be conceived. Similarly, intellect without
will, or will without intellect, is inconceivable. The relation
between the soul and its faculties is the same as the relation
existing between being and its transcendental attributes. Just
as being may be considered in a first moment—the metaphysical
moment, not the psychological moment—without its attributes,
so the soul may be considered in itself, apart from intellect
and will. But as soon as the necessary operations of the soul
are adverted to, the soul reveals itself to us as the synthesis of
intellect and will.[37]

There are definite advantages, remarks Duns Scotus, in conceiving the relationship between the soul and its faculties in
this fashion. The first of these advantages is an easier and
more simple explanation of man's rational activity. The upholders of a real distinction between the soul and its faculties
introduce into psychological life an unnecessary multiplicity
that impairs the nobility and perfection of the soul. A nature's
perfection is in fact measured by the acts that it is able to
perform by itself. Now if intellect and will are merely accidents
of the soul, it follows that the soul is unable of itself to think
and to will. And since man's happiness consists in knowledge
and love, intellect and will would, in such a case, find their
happiness in themselves, whereas the soul would attain its
happiness only through its faculties and *per accidens*.[38]

Another advantage to be drawn from the acceptance of a
formal distinction between the soul and its faculties is the

---

[37] "It must therefore be thought that the soul in the first moment,
as it were, of its essence is simply that particular nature, whereas in
the second moment it is operative, that is, capable of performing this
or that operation, and that the powers, which are precisely the principles of these operations, are contained *'unitive'* in the essence." *Ibid.*,
n. 18. The term *"unitive"* is reserved by Scotus to indicate the manner
in which two or more formalities are contained in one thing. The thing
is in relation to the formalities as the *tertium idem realiter*.

[38] *Ibid.*, n. 15.

clarification of certain points concerning those particular aspects on which stress is laid by the other solutions. That intellect and will appear to be *virtutes* or operative powers of the soul and have been thought of as mere accidents can be explained by the fact that, although not really distinct from the soul's essence, they are nevertheless *quasi passiones* or attributes of it. This same fact has been accounted for by philosophers who claim that intellect and will share in the nature of both substantial and accidental forms without being exactly either one. To say that intellect and will are parts of the soul, as some philosophers do, is not absolutely wrong. In fact, neither intellect nor will, taken alone, expresses the whole perfection of the soul. Furthermore, the formal distinction makes it plain that one faculty cannot be reduced to the perfection of the other, and much less to the perfection of the whole soul, even though each faculty is really identical with the soul.

St. Bonaventure calls intellect and will consubstantial forms of the soul. By this term he intends to emphasize the very special character of the relation between the soul and its faculties, which are not accidents of the soul, and yet do not constitute its essence, but can be identified with it only *"reductive."* If one compares St. Bonaventure's teaching with the doctrine of Duns Scotus on this score, he will not fail to agree with the following statement: Duns Scotus' doctrine is essentially an effort to determine in more precise and technical language the somewhat vague affirmations of the Seraphic Doctor. Hence his substitution of *quasi passiones animae* for the Bonaventurian *consubstantiales* and of *idem animae realiter, non tamen formaliter* for St. Bonaventure's *reductive.*

INTELLECT AND WILL

Another scholastic controversy worth mentioning, not so much because of its intrinsic importance as because of the opportunity it offers of emphasizing the directive lines of Scotistic thought, is the question of the relationship of dependence and superiority between intellect and will. It cannot be denied that the will does not move itself, that is to say, it does not determine itself to act, unless the intellect presents its object to it. The truth of the old scholastic saying, *Nihil volitum quin praecognitum,* is acknowledged by the Subtle Doctor. An act of the will is always preceded by an act of the intellect. However, some scholastics are inclined to see in this law of psychological dependence also a law of metaphysical dependence of the will on the intellect. The intellectual act would not only *precede* the volitional act, it would also be its cause. The volitional act is in the will, but not from the will: the efficient cause determining the act is the object present in the phantasm (Godfrey of Fontaines), or in the intellect (St. Thomas, Henry of Ghent).

"These two opinions," Duns Scotus points out, "agree in admitting that the will is moved by an extrinsic agent, but are at variance, as is evident, in specifying it." [39]

Duns Scotus thinks it necessary to depart from these points of view for two reasons. The first is this. The object influences the will in one way only: it either attracts or repels it. On the contrary, the proper characteristic of the will is its ability to determine itself either positively or negatively in regard to any object. This essential indetermination can be explained only by admitting that it is the will that actually determines itself to will or not to will. Secondly, an act that is received only passively must be called an act of the agent or of the cause that determines it, rather than an act of the recipient. Hence, if it were the object that determines the will to act, the whole effective causality of the volitional act should be attributed to the object. The act itself would become an act of the object rather than an act of the will.

---

[39] *Op. Oxon.,* II, d. 25, q. unica, n. 5.

The consequences following from such a doctrine are not difficult to see. Since the influence of the object upon the will is a natural, necessary one, i.e., such that it admits of only one direction, a psychological determinism will ensue that can hardly be reconciled with freedom.[40]

Hence, if it is right to recognize that the will does not determine itself to act prior to the presentation of the object on the part of the intellect, it must also be affirmed that the object so presented never necessarily determines the will to act or not to act. The last decision, the definitive one, belongs to the will. This amounts to saying that the principal efficient cause of the volitional act is the will itself, while the act of the intellect is only a necessary condition *(conditio sine qua non)* or, at most, a partial cause of it.[41]

On this premise, we are now able to make a further step and examine Duns Scotus' answer to another famous scholastic question: which faculty is superior, intellect or will *(utra potentia sit nobilior, intellectus an voluntas)*? Is man's highest perfection represented by intellectual activity or by the activity of the will? Duns Scotus approaches this problem with the greatest care. He devotes to it a special question, where he sets down very clearly, side by side, the arguments in favor of the primacy of the intellect and those in support of the primacy of the will.[42] Here we shall only touch upon the salient points of the discussion and the arguments of a purely philosophical nature.

From the intellect proceed not only intellective acts but also acts of the will, as the principle *nil volitum quin praecognitum* indicates. Hence the intellect, affirm the intellectualists, that is, the upholders of the primacy of the intellect, is an equivocal

---

[40] *Ibid.,* n. 6; IV, d. 49, q. ex latere, n. 17.

[41] *Op. Oxon.,* IV, q. ex latere, nn. 16-17. These terms will be explained in the following chapter.

[42] *Ibid.* See the whole question.

efficient cause as regards the volitional acts. But the equivocal efficient cause—a cause is called equivocal when it produces effects of a different nature from its own—is more perfect than its effects. Therefore, the intellect is more perfect than the will.

While internal experience, remarks Duns Scotus, tells us that every act of the will is preceded by knowledge, it also tells us that the will rules over all man's interior powers. It rules over memory by forcing it to recall things, and it rules over the intellect by forcing it to concentrate on one object rather than on another. Shall we not be authorized, then, to say that the will is the equivocal efficient cause, and therefore a more perfect cause, of the intellective acts? Actually, neither is the intellect the efficient and total, i.e., adequate, cause of the act of willing, nor is the will the efficient and total cause of the act of knowing. Both the act of the will and the act of the intellect are primarily acts of the faculty on whose causal efficiency they mainly depend. The truth is that both intellect and will exercise a certain causal influence on each other.

Yet intellect and will are not on the same plane. While the intellective act is subordinate to the volitive activity, insofar as it prepares it and thus becomes a subservient cause to the will (*causa subserviens voluntati*), the will commands the intellect as a superior commands an inferior. It is thus a superior cause in respect to the act of the intellect (*hoc modo voluntas imperans intellectui est causa superior respectu actus eius*).[43]

Intellectualists may object to this argument and say: we concede that the will can command the intellect. This fact, however, will never destroy the natural dependence that the volitive activity has on knowledge—a dependence that even the voluntarists are willing to admit. Now what depends on another is

---

[43] *Ibid.*, n. 16.

necessarily inferior to it in perfection. Hence the will is inferior to the intellect.

Duns Scotus' answer to this objection is that there are different kinds of dependence. Dependence in order of generation, for example, does not imply by any means a greater perfection in what precedes in relation to what comes afterwards. Again, the end comes last, and yet it is more perfect than what leads up to it. The form of material things depends on matter, yet it is superior to matter in perfection. The dependence of the will on the intellect is precisely a dependence of this kind: the volitional act comes after the intellective act because the latter is naturally ordered to the former, as means are ordered to end and matter to form. "In a generative succession things that come later depend on the preceding ones, and yet they are more perfect."[44] If the will existed as will in virtue of the intellect, its dependence would of course mean an inferiority of perfection. This is exactly what the position of the intellectualists amounts to. In fact, they observe, if by a pure hypothesis man were endowed with intellect alone, he would still be defined as a rational animal; but if he had will without intellect, he would *ipso facto* lose his dignity of rational being. Left to itself, will is nothing but an inclination similar to the tendency whereby heavy bodies fall towards their center of gravity.

To this Duns Scotus answers: "Even if love alone remained, it would not be merely a necessary tendency like gravitation, but an operation worthy of intellectual nature. In fact, to be an operation, and to be such an operation, [is something that] love does not derive from the intellect; rather it is so in conjunction with the intellect."[45]

From the foregoing discussion it seems clear that the basis of the whole controversy lies in different conceptions of will.

---

[44] *Ibid.,* n. 18.
[45] *Ibid.,* n. 17.

For Duns Scotus, man's will is rational by nature and does not derive such an essential characteristic from the intellect. Just as a thing cannot be separated from its own nature, so will and rationality are inseparable. Since no true rationality is possible without freedom, and since freedom is the proper characteristic of the volitive activity—knowledge in itself is not free, for it is necessarily determined by the object—it logically follows that the highest degree of human perfection lies in the will rather than in the intellect.

THE IMMORTALITY OF THE SOUL

Is the human soul immortal? Duns Scotus has no doubt that it is. However, he believes that a rigorous and apodictic demonstration of this doctrine is impossible. There are many persuasive arguments, of course, but none of them is so evident as to force our assent.[46]

Duns Scotus is fully aware of the gravity of such a position, which represents a break with the traditional teaching that had been painfully developed during the twelfth and thirteenth centuries. On the other hand, he does not seem to share our fear in denying to human reason the possibility of establishing by its own power such an important truth. Rather he finds in this deficiency a new motive for raising his mind to God and magnifying His mercy. "From this it appears how thankful we should be to God's bounty, who gave us through faith the greatest assurance about those things that concern our eternal destiny, and about which even the greatest minds can tell us almost nothing." [47]

In the middle ages, whenever a thinker wished to learn whether a certain truth could be attained by the light of reason or only by faith, he would consult, first of all, the works of Aristotle and see if the philosopher had known and taught it.

---

[46] *Op. Oxon.,* IV, d. 43, q. 2, n. 16.
[47] *Ibid.,* n. 33.

If he had, the question was looked upon as solved: reason itself could attain such a truth. If he had not, then a strong presumption, if not a decisive argument, would exist that the truth in question could not be attained by the light of reason unaided by revelation. That is why in the demonstration of the immortality of the soul, the Aristotelian texts that seemed to favor such a doctrine were usually brought forth.

With regard to Aristotle's thought on this point, Duns Scotus points out that, along with texts favoring the immortality of the soul, others exist which seem to indicate the Stagirite's opposite view. It must therefore be admitted that concerning the problem of the immortality of the soul, Aristotle did not have clear and definite ideas: sometimes he seems to favor it, at other times to deny it. At least it must be conceded that anyone wishing to base his convictions on Aristotle's works will find it difficult to make a clear-cut decision for or against the immortality of the soul.

The apparent contradiction of this double series of texts can perhaps be explained by the fact that Aristotle allowed himself to be dominated by the argument he was handling at each time, no matter whether the argument was more favorable to one side of the question or the other *(consonum uni parti magis quam alteri)*. However, to be more explicit, the reason for such a double stand lies in this: that the works of Aristotle, as the works of all philosophers, are not all of a purely philosophical character, nor are they a series of strictly rigorous arguments. There are usually weak points, that is, statements that logically are not very strong, or such that they have no other foundation than a certain probability and the support of preceding philosophers. "Sometimes philosophers are satisfied with personal convictions that are only probable, and sometimes with conclusions that do not follow necessarily from their principles." [48]

---

[48] *Ibid.,* n. 16.

In addition to the arguments from direct or indirect authority, arguments from reason are usually brought forth in support of the immortality of the soul. Of these arguments some are along the lines of the Aristotelian trend of thought, others are more in conformity with the Augustinian doctrine. Let us consider Duns Scotus' criticism of both types of arguments, beginning with those mentioned by St. Thomas.

As is well known, the Angelic Doctor proves the immortality of the soul from its spirituality. A thing can be corrupted either because of the internal dissolution of the parts that compose it (corruption *per se*), or because of the loss of the indispensable support for its *esse* (corruption *per accidens*). But the human soul can be corrupted in neither way. It cannot be corrupted *per accidens,* for being independent of the body in its operations, it must also be independent in its *esse*. The *esse* of the soul separated from the body is identical with the *esse* of the soul united to it. The only difference is that in this latter case the soul participates or communicates its own *esse* to the body. It can be easily understood, then, that the body can be separated from the soul without prejudicing the soul's existence.

The soul cannot be corrupted *per se,* because it is simple. To perish, the soul would have to separate itself from itself, from its own *esse;* it would have to destroy itself, which is just as impossible as to give to itself its own *esse*.

In the first place, Duns Scotus does not agree with the statement that the soul has the *esse per se* in the Thomistic sense, which implies the identification of the *esse* of the soul with the *esse* of the whole, i.e., of the human composite. No doubt the soul has its own reality, its own *esse* distinct from the *esse* of the body. But insofar as the soul is the form of the body with which it constitutes the human composite, its *esse* is not definitive but ordered to the *esse* of the whole, which results precisely from the union of the *esse animae* with the *esse corporis.*[49] Accordingly, the soul has the *esse per se,* as all real things do, if by the term *esse* is meant the act by which a thing exists outside its cause; it does not have the *esse per se,* if by this is meant the ultimate and definitive act by which a thing exists in its natural concreteness. In other words, the *esse per se* belongs to the human composite and not to the soul.

The soul, however, is different from other forms, "because it is not immersed in matter, nor is it totally absorbed by it," as manifested by the fact "that it possesses operations and energies that are proper to itself, independently of the body."[50] Hence it is not corruptible *per accidens* as other forms are.

Thus Duns Scotus acknowledges the incorruptibility of the soul *per accidens,* but not on the ground of the Thomistic principle that the *esse* of the soul is identical with the *esse* of the whole—this will afford proof that the soul *can* be immortal, but not that it is *de facto* immortal. What prevents the transition from mere possibility to actuality is the fact that the soul is by nature ordered to the *esse* of the whole composite, and the suspension of this order or natural law cannot be demonstrated by the light of reason alone. Every suspension of a natural law is a miracle, and a miracle is not something that happens of necessity. Hence, from the fact that the *esse* of the soul does not depend on the *esse* of the body, one cannot draw the conclusion that the soul has therefore its *esse* without the body.[51]

To insist on the fact that in knowledge the soul acts independently of matter, at least to a certain extent, and to conclude from this to its separate existence, is no better argument. If it is true that the soul is the proximate subject of the rational act, it is also true that it is man, the whole man, that understands through the soul, his form. The act of understanding,

---

[49] *Quodlibet.,* q. 9, n. 15.
[50] *Ibid.,* n. 8.
[51] *Op. Oxon.,* IV, d. 43, q. 2, n. 23.

as all other acts, is primarily an act of the *suppositum,* and the *suppositum* is not the soul but the whole human compound, even though it is because of the soul, an immaterial form, that man is endowed with rational activity.

Here again we must take notice of the soul's natural ordination to the composite. Philosophy cannot go further than that. The fact that the soul, once it is separated from the body, can understand is known to us only by faith.[52] It is only by identifying the *esse* of the soul with the *esse* of the whole that this is possible; however, as already proved, the *esse animae* is not the *esse totius.*

The argument which attempts to demonstrate the essential incorruptibility of the soul is likewise defective. True, the soul is an immaterial and simple form which cannot be corrupted through the separation of parts; but it can be destroyed and annihilated by God. The soul is indestructible by intrinsic causes and by inferior extrinsic causes, but not by a superior extrinsic cause. God can always do what is not absurd and implies no contradiction.

In conclusion, Duns Scotus admits the incorruptibility (in the exact sense of possibility of incorruption) of the soul *per accidens;* but because of his own particular notions of form and the union of soul and body, he refutes the argument by which St. Thomas tries to prove the impossibility for the soul to be corrupted with the body. Likewise, he admits the incorruptibility of the soul *per se* as a possibility, but because of his own conception of the relationship between divine will and created things—this is to be expounded in another chapter—he denies that the actual immortality of the soul can be established on the basis of evident, or at least necessary, reasons. For him the only legitimate conclusion is this: the human soul by its nature can be immortal.

---

[52] *Quodlibet.,* q. 9, n. 14.

Evidently, the basic reasoning in Scotus' criticism of the two Thomistic arguments is essentially the same. However, the rejection of the first argument entails more complex considerations.

The favorite argument of the Augustinian school is based on man's natural desire for immortality. Duns Scotus thinks that this argument is too vague. If such a desire were truly natural, no doubt it would constitute a solid foundation for demonstrating the immortality of the human soul. But in order to know that such a desire is truly natural, it is necessary first to know that it is truly grounded in human nature. This is equivalent to saying that we must first demonstrate that man is by nature destined to be immortal. In such a case, we would assume as already demonstrated what the argument is supposed to prove.

On the other hand, if by natural desire is meant that spontaneous joy with which man welcomes any promise of immortality *(actus elicitus)*, then it must be said that, while it is comparatively easy to ascertain by experience the existence of such a desire in us, it is not so easy to demonstrate that the desire in question is the expression of a natural tendency. It must first be established on good, solid grounds, as previously stated, that the soul has a natural capacity for immortality and is naturally destined to it.

The same remarks are made by Duns Scotus on the other Augustinian argument, based on man's desire for a supreme, and therefore everlasting, happiness. The validity of this argument rests on the possibility of demonstrating by arguments deduced from reason alone that the beatific vision of God is the end of man.[53] This demonstration is understandable to one who admits that God is the proper object of the human intellect, but not to Duns Scotus. From the fact that the proper

---

[53] "For it must be known to us by natural reason that that act befits us as our own end." *Op. Oxon.*, IV, d. 43, q. 2, n. 32.

object of the human intellect is being as being, it does not
follow that we must know God perfectly; a conceptual knowledge of Him is sufficient. If God were the proper object of
our intellect, man would be made, as it were, on a divine pattern that would demand his immortality. But this is not the
case, and so no argument for the immortality of the soul can
be built on that premise.

IV

KNOWLEDGE

Man is in a continuous becoming. He develops his vegetative, sensitive, intellectual, and volitional powers only by coming in contact with things. Thus the human body attains its perfection by utilizing the things that surround it in a series of processes, of which the most characteristic is nutrition. This is not difficult to understand, since we have here things of the same nature. More mysterious is the relation between soul and things, between spirit and matter, which are so different from one another. All the difficulties center on the fact of knowledge, for it is through knowledge that things become ours in a very special way and nourish, as it were, our soul's life.

The problem of knowledge consists not so much in discovering the process by which man knows, as in determining the roles that both soul and things play in causing the cognitive act. All becoming finds its explanation in the interplay of the four causes, i.e., material, formal, efficient, and final. Scholastics in general agree in maintaining that the material cause of the cognitive act is sense or intellect, the formal cause is respectively the sensible species and the intelligible species, and the final cause the perfection which is naturally due to man. Disagreement starts when the efficient cause is to be determined. It is the purpose of this chapter to examine, on the basis of Scotistic texts, the fundamental points of the controversy. This will provide the opportunity for pointing out Duns Scotus' speculative contribution to the solution of the problem of knowledge.

SENSATION

The first cognitive contact between man and things is through the senses. Duns Scotus endorses and makes his own the doctrine of the psychological structure of sensation, as formulated by the Aristotelian school. According to this doctrine, man has five senses, each of them with a particular organ which is modified directly or indirectly by external bodies. The common or central sense has the task of coordinating the data of the external senses. Sensation consists essentially in a modification of the organs produced by the action of an external body upon them. By Duns Scotus and all scholastic philosophers this modification is called *species sensibilis*.

Duns Scotus' agreement with the Aristotelian school comes to an end when the question arises whether in sensation the soul is active or passive. Many Aristotelians used to take literally the Stagirite's saying that *sentire est quoddam pati;* consequently, they attributed to the external body all the efficient causality of sensation. Duns Scotus is of a different opinion. He believes that the sensitive power is not merely passive. For him sensation can only be explained by the active concurrence of both the external body and the sensitive power. Since the arguments on which he founds his opinion on the nature of the concurrence in question are the same for sensation and intellection, they will be considered later when intellection is discussed.

Sensation brings man in contact with material things and makes him know them in their immediate, physical reality. This kind of knowledge man has in common with all other animals. However, man has a much more perfect knowledge of things; he has intellectual knowledge, which transcends sensible knowledge and is of a different nature. Through intellectual knowledge man knows things in their essence and in their causes; at least to a certain extent, he discovers the meaning and the intimate structure of things and the relations that bind everything into a unique system of reality. This is possible to us insofar as we rise from the particular to the universal. The transition from sensible knowledge to intellectual knowledge is done through the process of abstraction.

THE DOCTRINE OF ABSTRACTION

The various steps in the abstractive process, as described by the Aristotelian school, are well known. Things exist as singular, and as such they reveal themselves to the senses through the sensible species. The intellect, however, knows them through the concept, which is universal. Thus universality is synonymous with intelligibility. To ask, then, how things become intelligible is equivalent to asking how do concepts become universal. The transformation is effected by the intellect, more specifically by the agent intellect, which, by illuminating the phantasm, strips it of its individuating notes and produces a new species. This is called the intelligible species, because in it the thing takes on the characteristics of universality and becomes intelligible, that is, knowable to the intellect.

In Duns Scotus' philosophy the abstractive process can also be resolved into the traditional Aristotelian elements. The starting point is the particular concrete thing offered by the phantasm and the result is the intelligible species, while the act of mediation between the two is performed by the agent intellect. Yet, when carefully studied, the Scotistic abstraction reveals at every step the new spirit of the system to which it belongs. Let us examine it from its very starting point, the thing and its phantasm.

The phantasm, like the thing from which it is produced, is singular; but for Duns Scotus the structure of the singular is certainly not such as to be in perfect agreement with the Aristotelian teaching. In fact, as we have already proved in the course of this study, the individual is for Duns Scotus the synthesis of a common nature and haecceity. It may be objected: if in the concrete thing there actually is a nature distinct from the individuating element, will not that action by which the intellect strips a nature of its individuating notes be useless? Will not the nature be grasped directly in the phantasm?

To this objection Duns Scotus answers by recalling his own theory of common nature. This nature, he says, is common, but not universal; it is the real foundation for universality but not universality itself. The action of the agent intellect is required precisely for the transformation of the physical universal into a metaphysical universal. The cause by which an object obtains that positive indetermination in the intellect that makes it truly universal—an indetermination which is greater than the negative indetermination proper to common nature—cannot be the object itself, but the agent intellect in virtue of its universalizing power.

How is this universalizing action of the agent intellect to be understood? For one who maintains that everything that exists in concrete reality is individual, and only individual, the action of the agent intellect cannot be understood otherwise than as a process by which the thing is stripped of its individuating notes. This is done by the active intellect in the act by which it sheds its own light upon the sensible phantasm.

Against this way of conceiving abstraction Duns Scotus proposes two fundamental objections. If the thing is individual, and only individual, he observes, I do not see how it can become universal as the result of pure illumination. When I illumine a thing, I see better what the thing is in all its particular details; no light, however, can bring forth what is not in the thing itself. In order that the illuminating action of the agent intellect may be able to universalize, one must admit that there already exists in the thing the universal as such. The fact that the universal is there in a more or less hidden state, so that it can be brought to light only by the revealing action of the intellect, by no means modifies its nature as a universal. Hence one of two things follows. Either the first alternative is true, namely, that the thing is only individual and in no way contains the universal, and then we head toward nominalism, which makes the universal a fiction of the intellect. In this case the intellect is fully credited with the formation of the concept. Or the second alternative is admitted, namely, that the universal exists as such in the thing, and then we fall into the theory of Platonic ideas. The only difference is that the universal essences, instead of being placed in a transcendental world, are to be found in the very heart of sensible reality.

The theory of common nature is, in Scotus' opinion, the only theory that can save us from the two extremes of nominalism and exaggerated realism. The nature is a potential universal which receives its ultimate actuality as a universal from the intellect. In this case, however, abstraction must be conceived in a somewhat different manner. It will no longer be a question of an illuminating action of the agent intellect upon the phantasm, from which the intelligible species or universal in act would, as it were, come forth; instead, there will be an effective collaboration between the object present in the phantasm and the intellect in the production of the idea. Through the phantasm, the object draws the attention of the intellect upon the nature, which of itself is indifferent to singularity or universality. This nature, upon entering the intentional order, acquires the modality proper to this order, namely, universality, and thus becomes intelligible. The universalizing action of the agent intellect consists precisely in this: to endow nature with this new modality. The result of this action is the production of the intelligible species in the possible intellect.

The reasons that led Duns Scotus to admit this intentional entity called intelligible species are manifold, and they are fully explained in one of the questions in the *Opus Oxoniense*.[54] The principal argument is based on a phenomenological study of our intellective act. There is a moment in which the object is indifferent and of no interest to our intellect. To this a second moment succeeds, in which the object stirs up our intellective power and moves it to understand it. The act by which the object is actually understood represents the third moment: the intellect takes possession of the object and becomes intentionally the object itself.

A reason must be found for the transition from the first moment, when the object has not as yet stirred up the attention of the intellect, to the second moment, in which the intellect is moved to understand it. Evidently, a change has taken place. The object, of course, did not undergo any change, for it is the same object before and after it is known. Has the phantasm changed? Certainly not. Any change within the phantasm will always be of a sensible order, and the object, despite all possible changes in the phantasm, will never be transferred to the order of intelligibility. Nor is any change possible in the agent intellect, for nothing can be received in the agent *(nihil recipitur in agente)*. Thus of all the factors concurring to the intellective act, namely, object, phantasm, agent intellect, and possible intellect, only this last can be held responsible for the change by which a thing passes from its remote potentiality of intelligibility to its proximate poten-

---

[54] *Op. Oxon.*, I, d. 3, q. 6.

tiality of being understood. What is the new fact that has taken place? It is the production of the intelligible species. By combining their powers, agent intellect and phantasm produce within the possible intellect, which acts as a material cause, a special entity that is a *similitudo,* or the intentional correspondent of the real object in *esse intelligibili* and in *esse objectivo.*[55]

At this point the question naturally arises: what causes the nature, which in reality is only a *natura communis,* to become *universal* in the intentional order?[56] This cause cannot be the object, since this reveals itself only as it is; nor can it be the intellect as passive faculty, for as such it receives but does not transform. The cause in question can therefore only be the intellect as an agent, and precisely in its capacity as agent intellect. "To explain why the agent intellect, together with common nature, makes the object universal, there is but one reason: the intellect is that kind of a power. In like manner fire heats because it is fire." [57]

It can only be regretted that in his analysis of the process of universalization Duns Scotus stops here. Had he taken the lead from his own theory of the proper object of the intellect, namely, being as being—a theory that, as previously demonstrated, includes a virtual innatism of the idea of being—he

---

[55] *Ibid.,* n. 16: "The way I understand it is this. In the first moment of the process the object, either by itself or through its phantasm, is present to the agent intellect. In the second moment, in which they [the object and the agent intellect] are present as active cause to the possible intellect, which is therefore acted upon, the *species* is produced in the possible intellect. Finally, in the third moment, the object is through the species present as intelligible."

[56] *Metaph.* VII, q. 18, n. 8: "But what is the cause of that indetermination by which the object, as soon as it is known, becomes completely universal?"

[57] *Ibid.*

could have given a more precise and profound answer to the problem at issue.[58]

To fix the precise points of difference between Aristotelian abstraction and Scotistic abstraction, the following statements are in order:

1. The distance between the starting point and the point of arrival in Aristotle's abstractive process is greater than that in Duns Scotus' process. While for Aristotle the process of abstraction begins with the singular, for Duns Scotus it starts with common nature, which keeps a perfect balance between singularity and universality.

2. However, when the intellect's contribution to universalization is considered, one must say that the parts are inverted. The step from common nature to the universal is shorter, but it is mainly the task of the intellect. While it is true that in the Aristotelian system the step from the singular to the universal is longer, it is likewise true that the action of the intellect is less important. In fact, the intellect merely points out by its light the universal or the form that is in the things. It does not contribute anything of its own, nor does it communicate its nature to the idea, as Scotus teaches. Scotus says in effect that universality is a new modality that the intellect itself confers upon the object.

3. Thus for Duns Scotus abstraction is not properly speaking a dematerialization of the object, or an act by which the form is set free from the individuating notes rooted in matter; rather it is an act by which the object takes up a new way of being, is raised to the order of intelligibility, or the ideal order, and acquires the note of universality. In this sense, it must be recog-

---

[58] For Rosmini the light of the agent intellect is the innate idea of being. To universalize is for him nothing but to see a thing in the light of the possible being. Cf. *Nuovo saggio sull'origine delle idee,* vol. II, 2nd part, chap. 3, art. 2. In my opinion this Rosminian theory can be considered as a development and integration of the Scotistic doctrine of abstraction.

nized, the activity of the intellect is for Duns Scotus more decisive and efficacious.

THE EFFICIENT CAUSE OF KNOWLEDGE

To abstract is not yet to understand. The intellective act consists, properly speaking, in the living synthesis of the object, present in the intelligible species, with the intellect. It is from this synthesis that the concept or idea, the *verbum mentale,* of the thing known is generated.

Here again the problem arises: is understanding an act of the soul only because it is received in the intellective faculty, or is it an act of the soul also because it is produced by the intellective faculty? In other words, is the intellect only the material cause of the new reality, the intellective act, or is it also the efficient cause of it? Duns Scotus, as usual, is confronted with a variety of solutions of the problem which he has to face and evaluate. This he does in a remarkable question of his principal work,[59] where he makes us assist at a debate between a psychology of knowledge of Platonic-Augustinian tendencies and a psychology of knowledge of the Aristotelian trend of thought. He listens patiently to the reasons of both contendants, and then, calling all back to the real point of controversy, which is the act of knowing, he remarks that none of the suggested theories gives a sufficient reason for all the experimental data encountered in human knowledge. Hence he proposes a new solution, which, he believes, is more logical and consistent. We are now going to take part in this debate, and we may judge for ourselves who is the winner.

The Platonic-Augustinian Theory. As usual, Duns Scotus chooses Henry of Ghent as the exponent of the Platonic-

---

[59] *Op. Oxon.,* I, d. 3, q. 7: "Utrum pars intellectiva, vel aliquid eius sit causa gignens vel ratio gignendi notitiam actualem."

Augustinian school. The thesis that Henry of Ghent proposes
to demonstrate is formulated by the Subtle Doctor in these
terms: "Concerning this question, there is an opinion that attributes the whole activity of understanding to the soul alone.
This opinion is attributed to St. Augustine." [60] According to
this view, the only real efficient cause of the cognitive act is
the intellect. The demonstration is based mainly on the two
following arguments. In the first place, one cannot deny the
fact that the act of understanding is a spiritual act, an act
that belongs to the very life of our soul. Likewise, the principle
must be admitted that no effect can be more perfect than its
cause. Now, if the object and not our intellective faculty were
the cause of the act of understanding, such an act could not
be called a living act of our soul. Furthermore, we would run
into the absurdity of having an effect superior to its cause.

In the second place, the act of understanding is an immanent
operation: it would not be such if it were not an act of the
faculty in which it is immanent. Moreover, the act is of the
one who performs it, not of him who receives it. Hence, if
the intellective act were the product of something extrinsic
to the knowing faculty, that is, of the object, it would no longer
be possible to speak of an immanent operation. The act itself,
rather than an act of the soul, should be called an act of the
object, which is evidently false. The act of understanding is
therefore an act of the soul not only because it takes place
in the soul, but also because it comes *from the soul.*

As to the role which the object plays in the production of
the intellective act, Henry of Ghent, says Duns Scotus, has
no clear idea. Sometimes he speaks in terms of a *causa sine qua
non;* at other times he states that the object present in the phantasm has the role of stimulating and disposing the intellect to

---

[60] *Ibid.,* n. 2.

know. Thus, rather than a cause, the external object must be called *the occasion* for the act of understanding, an occasion, though, that is indispensable for the performance of the act.

In Duns Scotus' opinion this way of reasoning runs against insuperable difficulties. The principal difficulty will be clear from a simple reflection upon the metaphysical doctrine of the four causes. All reality can be sufficiently explained through its four causes. When the four causes are present and not impeded, the effect will follow necessarily in the case of natural causes; if all or one of the causes is free, the effect may also follow. For that matter, it is enough that the efficient cause and the material cause be present in perfect condition in order to produce the effect. This is possible because the form, inasmuch as it is the terminus of the production, is somehow contained in the efficient cause; the final cause in turn is either a consequence of the production, or, if it precedes it, it is simply the motive that moves the efficient cause with which it can be identified. The formal and final causes are thus but perfections which complete and integrate the efficient cause. A perfect efficient cause and an adequate material cause are, alone, the fundamental efficient causes of a reality.

Now, if we apply this doctrine to the fact of knowledge as understood by Henry of Ghent, we will see immediately the weak point in his theory. For him the soul is by itself the efficient cause of the act of understanding. It is also its material cause, inasmuch as it is the recipient of the very act of understanding. Thus in the soul alone we would have all that is required for knowledge: the concurrence of a perfect efficient cause and of a sufficiently adequate material cause. This concurrence, precisely because it is rooted in the very nature of the soul, is continuous. The effect, then, must also be continuous, which is equivalent to saying that the soul will be constantly thinking and understanding. It would at least be constantly thinking of, and understanding, itself. This is in contrast with our own experience, which tells us that the intellective act takes place only when the soul is presented with an object.

To explain this necessary dependence of the intellective act upon its object by saying that the presence of the object is a *conditio sine qua non,* or the indispensable occasion for the act of understanding, amounts to this: either the soul is an efficient cause which is both imperfect and insufficient, or, in addition to the four causes, there must be a fifth cause. If Henry of Ghent accepts the first alternative, he destroys his own theory; if he accepts the second alternative, he puts himself in contrast with the common doctrine and the truth.

But there are other difficulties. If the intellective act is the product of the soul alone, how shall we explain the fact that the idea is an image *(similitudo)* of the object, whose nature it reveals in the intentional order? Only a causal dependence can explain the dependence *in esse* of one thing upon another. Moreover, the intellective act is the more perfect as its object is more perfect. It is on the basis of this principle that Aristotle affirms that happiness consists in the knowledge of God. If the object were not concurring as a true and proper cause in the production of the act of knowledge and the whole causality were due to our intellect, the greater or lesser perfection of the act would no longer be proportioned to the object known, but only to the greater or lesser intensity of the power I put into the act of knowledge. Consequently, the act by which I know a fly could be equally perfect with, or even more perfect than, the act by which I know God.

On the other hand, if the theory of Henry of Ghent were correct, one should conclude that the activity of our intellect is infinite. Two things are in effect worth noting: first, that our intellect is capable of knowing an infinite number of things, and hence is capable of infinite acts of understanding;

second, that each act of knowledge presupposes a limited amount of activity and perfection. To infinite perfections must therefore correspond infinite amounts of activity. If the whole activity of knowing belonged to the intellect, the human intellect would have an infinite activity, and hence an infinite perfection. We would then have the absurdity of an infinite in potency.

The Aristotelian-Thomistic Theory. Let us now turn to the defenders of the psychology of knowledge of the Aristotelian school. Duns Scotus here takes into consideration the doctrines of Godfrey of Fontaines, Giles of Rome, and St. Thomas Aquinas. Their basic tenets are grounded in metaphysics. Human knowledge is a movement, or rather a passage, from potentiality to actuality. As such, it is subject to the laws of becoming. The fundamental law of becoming is this: *quidquid movetur ab alio movetur,* which means that the passive principle and the active principle of movement must be distinct and different from one another. That our intellect is the passive principle in the act of understanding is granted by everyone. Thus, on the basis of the aforesaid law, it cannot be at the same time the active principle of understanding. Accordingly, the active principle must be distinct from our soul and can only be the object—unless we wish to admit the intervention of God or of the Intelligence of Arabian philosophy.

Further, every act of understanding is a reality within the order of the intelligibles *(in genere intelligibilium).* Just as in the order of beings *(in genere entium)* a reality results from the union of matter and form, so also in the intentional order, where the human intellect functions as matter. As primary matter is pure potentiality in the real order, so the intellect is pure potentiality or *tabula rasa* in the intentional order. In an analogous manner, just as the actuality of beings is from the form, so the whole actuality of understanding is from the species, which unites itself to our intellect and determines it to act.*

To Duns Scotus this way of conceiving the intellective act seems to be an assault on the dignity of the human soul. His criticism flows so naturally from his pen as to leave no doubt of his aversion for such a theory. "How would reasoning be possible? How would reflection be possible? How would the relations of reason or logical intentions arise? How would it be possible to maintain as true a false statement if the intelligible species generated by the phantasm were the only formal reason for any act of understanding?" [61] If the entire actuality of the act of understanding is on the part of the object, our faculty will be left with no initiative whatsoever in regard to ideas. It will not even be able to modify or elaborate what it receives from the object: it will be receptive, and nothing else. Yet it is plain that the object, of itself, can furnish the intellect only with the intelligible species; it cannot supply it with the notion of their relationship or any further logical development that the intelligible species receive in the intellect. In such a case knowledge would be nothing but the mirroring of reality. It would be hard to understand how it could be the organization and unification of reality through reasoning

---

* The accuracy of Duns Scotus' presentation of the Aristotelian-Thomistic view on the role that the object and the possible intellect play in knowledge may be questioned. Thus, although St. Thomas speaks repeatedly of possible intellect as a passive and receptive power (cf., for example, *Sum. Theol.,* I, q. 79, a. 2 c; *ibid.,* a. 4, ad 4; *ibid.,* a. 7 c), he credits it with the production of the *species intelligibilis expressa* or *verbum mentis.* However, it must be admitted that in their explanation of the process of ideogenesis, both St. Thomas and the followers of the Aristotelian school lay emphasis on the active role of the object and the agent intellect, which they consider as the principal causes of knowledge. Duns Scotus is for a more active role of the possible intellect. (*Tr.*)

[61] *Op. Oxon.,* I, d. 3, q. 7, nn. 11 and 16.

and the logical intentions which follow upon the intellect's reflection on the *apprehensio*. There would be no place for error, for error is not to be found in apprehension or the simple grasping of the object but in the judgment and its development through reasoning.

Nor is it possible to escape this conclusion by appealing to the activity of the agent intellect in the abstractive process. This activity is only an illumination of the phantasm directed to discovering and bringing forth into light the universal which is already contained implicitly in the object itself. Only the Scotistic abstraction contains virtually and makes possible such developments, not the kind of abstraction that is understood by strict Aristotelians. For the Scotistic abstraction is the result of an initiative that the intellect takes in regard to the object upon which it confers the new character of universality which the object, of itself, does not and cannot possess.

In addition to the foregoing considerations, it should be borne in mind that if the object were to determine our faculty to understand, one could no longer say, strictly speaking, that understanding is an act of our faculty. An example will clarify our point. The heating or burning of a piece of wood in contact with fire is the manifestation of a perfection that is in the fire, not in the piece of wood; for it is an essential property of fire to warm, whereas it is purely accidental for a piece of wood to undergo the action of the fire. If it were true that the whole actuality of understanding belonged to the object, our intellect would have the same relationship to understanding as wood to burning. We would then be able to say that our intellect understands, not because of an inherent, active capacity to assimilate things intentionally, but because of the capacity of the object to make itself understood. Thus the act of understanding would be a perfection of the object rather than a perfection of the soul.[62]

---

[62] *Ibid.*, nn. 9 and 17.

There is another datum of our internal experience that seems to conflict with the Aristotelian-Thomistic theory. When two men are presented with the same object, one man may get a better understanding of it than the other, depending on the capacity of his intellect, as well as the greater or lesser amount of attention that he gives to it. If my intellective act depended entirely on the object for its production, its degree of perfection could no longer depend on the different capacity of the intellect, nor could it depend on the greater or lesser effort on the part of him who understands: an object would be understood in an equal manner by everyone.[63] Likewise, it would be impossible to explain the formation within us of any intellective *habitus,* which makes easier and more effective the mind's conative act in the acquisition of knowledge. "Similarly, how can it be stated, without degrading the soul, that the phantasm produces effectively that natural action of the soul which is this latter's specific perfection?" [64] This observation holds true also for any doctrine that would substitute for the phantasm the intelligible species or the object in general.

Duns Scotus' aim in this series of arguments is to vindicate the nobility and perfection of the soul. He is rightly convinced that in the system of those who overstress the passivity of the intellect, the soul's nobility and perfection are greatly impaired, if not completely destroyed.

Here the critical part of Scotus' argumentation ends and its constructive part begins.

Duns Scotus' Theory. Anyone who wishes to give a satisfactory explanation of the intellective act, Duns Scotus points out, must keep before himself two equally important facts. The first is this: for us, understanding is a transition from potentiality to actuality, and so it demands an active efficient

---

[63] *Ibid.*, n. 17.
[64] *Ibid.*, n. 11

cause. The second fact is that man understands whenever he wishes to, so that in the act of understanding there is some kind of initiative on our part. This amounts to saying that the efficient cause of the act of understanding must somehow be placed also within us, for the will has no power over what does not belong to the soul. The theories previously examined are unacceptable; they run into many difficulties because their proponents did not take into due account these two facts. In his theory, Henry of Ghent well explains the second fact, namely the dependence of the intellect on some initiative of our soul, but does not sufficiently explain the first fact. Aristotelians explain the first fact but not the second one. "This will therefore be the solution of the problem: if neither the soul nor the object alone can be the total cause of the intellective act, and if only these two are required for the act of understanding, it follows that both factors taken together are the integral cause of knowledge."[65]

"Here again it seems that both the soul and the object present [to it] must concur together to form the intelligible species, or else the object is not present as an intelligible object." [66] But how is this "concurrence" of soul and the object to be understood, in order that they may constitute the adequate efficient cause of the intellective act? Duns Scotus is almost lavish in his explanations. He knows that he is propounding a new doctrine,[67] and so he formulates it with great accuracy.

The common doctrine distinguishes four causes: material, formal, efficient, and final. However, an effect does not always

---

[65] *Ibid.*, n. 20.

[66] *Ibid.*

[67] As I tried to prove in my essay, "Rapporti dottrinali fra Matteo d'Acquasparta e Giovanni Duns Scoto," *Studi Francescani,* ser. 3.a, XV (1943), 113-30, this doctrine, although formulated philosophically by the Subtle Doctor, was already implicitly contained in the Augustinian ideology, or at least in St. Bonaventure and Matthew of Acquasparta. It is therefore a new doctrine, but not in the fullest sense of the term.

have just one efficient cause; often the efficient causes are two.
In this case the efficacy of the efficient cause results from the
sum-total of the causality of two partial efficient causes. The
relationship between these two partial efficient causes is not
always the same. They may be related to one another essentially
or accidentally. Causes accidentally related to one another differ
from those which are essentially related in a three-fold manner.
In causes related essentially: (1) the second cause depends on
the first one for its causation; (2) one is more perfect than
the other; (3) they must always act simultaneously. On the
other hand, causes related accidentally: (1) have their own
causality independently of one another; (2) they are on the
same plane of perfection; (3) they can act successively. The
root of these differences lies in this: while the concurrence of
causes which are accidentally related can be eliminated by
proportionally increasing the power of one of them—a very
strong horse can pull a load that takes two horses of ordinary
strength—the case of the essentially related causes is quite
different. Among these the efficiency of one, no matter how
much it may be increased, never eliminates the need for the
action of the other. Thus no matter how perfect a man may
be, he will never be able to do without a woman in the process
of generation.

In turn, the essential subordination of two partial efficient
causes presents a two-fold possibility. Of the two causes concurring together to the production of a single effect, it may
happen that one receives its causality from the other (the cue
moves the ball only insofar as it is moved by the hand), or it
may also be that each one of the two causes is a cause in its
own right, independently of the other. This is what happens
in the process of generation, where neither the generative
power of the male depends on the female element, nor that
of the female depends on the male. Each element brings its
own original necessary contribution, in such a way that neither
can act without the concurrence of the other. It is within this

type of partial efficient causes that the collaboration between intellect and object in the production of the intellective act must be placed. The act of understanding is the result of these two factors, which concur in its production as two partial efficient causes essentially related to one another, each one having a causal efficiency proportioned to its own nature. Intellect and object "are therefore causes essentially related in this last manner, that is to say, one is simply more perfect than the other, but in such wise that both are perfect and independent of one another insofar as their own causality is concerned." [68]

Of the two causes, intellect and object, the more active, the one upon which rests greater responsibility, or, as Duns Scotus says, the *causa principalior* of the act of understanding, is the intellect. This is not only because the intellect is by nature more perfect than the material object, but also because in every case the act of understanding depends principally on our faculty. The reasons for this causal superiority of the intellect over the object are easy to understand; yet Duns Scotus does not fail to point them out in a very short question of the *Opus Oxoniense*.[69]

The first reason is that the object concurs effectively only in the production of that intellective act which has reference to itself, whereas our intellective faculty, inasmuch as it is the indispensable cause for all possible intellective acts, which are infinite or limitless, is in some way an unlimited active power. The second reason stems from the peculiar character of our understanding, which Duns Scotus never fails to stress: its vitality. The act of understanding, precisely because it is a vital act, is above all an act of our soul. When the object is said to act together with the intellect, the expression "act together" means really "to help." Evidently, the one who helps

[68] *Op. Oxon.,* I, d. 3, q. 7, n. 21.
[69] *Ibid.,* q. 8.

is never the principal agent, even if in a particular case his help is necessary. In emphasizing this point Duns Scotus goes so far as to assert that the object is almost like an instrument of the intellect *(quasi instrumentum ipsius intellectus)*.[70]

The study of Duns Scotus' doctrine on partial efficient causes has definite advantages. Among other things, it helps us understand the roles played respectively by the object presented by the intellect and the will in the volitional act, the thing and the sensitive faculty in sensation, and the phantasm and the agent intellect in the production of the intelligible species. These are all cases in which the collaboration between two partial efficient causes explained above is concretely realized.[71] The consequence of this Scotistic theory is that the activity of our intellect is given more emphasis. Through it, we realize more clearly that the act of understanding depends principally on the subject, not on the object.

Against such an activistic conception of the human intellect stands the authority of Aristotle, who affirms that *intelligere est pati*. Duns Scotus, the child of his times, cannot easily bear the thought of being in disagreement with the Stagirite, and he tries to give to Aristotle's statement an interpretation that is compatible with his own doctrine. Aristotle, he says, speaks here of the powers of the soul considered from a particular point of view. To grasp the exact meaning of his statements, one must always turn to his teaching as a whole and the general context from which the statements are taken. All acts of our powers can be considered either in the moment they are being formed, or in the moment they are received, as it were, into our soul once they are completed. As regards the acts considered in this second moment, our powers are

---

[70] *Ibid.,* n. 2.

[71] This Scotistic theory can also find its application in the solution of other problems, such as the collaboration between soul and body, will and grace, the individual and society.

passive. The acts are in effect received into the power concerned as its determinations or perfections, and are related to it as form is to matter. When Aristotle states that *intelligere est pati,* he does not consider the intellective act in the moment it is being formed through the concomitant action of the intellect and the object, but only in the moment in which it is received as a perfection of the intellect. This evidently leaves intact the question of the activity or nonactivity of the intellect in the production of the cognitive act, when this latter is considered as a complete process and not just as a particular moment of it. To be sure, Aristotle never says that the intellect is an efficient cause of the act of understanding, and we have seen the reason for it. It is also true that he never says that the intellect is in no way active. In their interpretation of his thought Aristotelians go further than Aristotle himself and make him responsible for statements he never made.[72]

Yet Duns Scotus does not want to take a definite stand, and makes certain reservations on the validity of his Aristotelian exegesis: *"hic tamen non determinando dico quod Philosophus locutus est, etc."* [73] In other words, this is an acceptable interpretation aiming at the reconciliation of Aristotle's thought with his own theory. In the supposition that Aristotle had a different point of view, Duns Scotus is not thereby willing to sacrifice his own solution of the problem at issue, for to him it has all the appearances of a true solution. This is a wonderful example of Duns Scotus' evaluation of the arguments from authority and of his attitude toward Aristotle.

---

[72] "These quotations, therefore, point to the fact that the intellect is passive, for they do not consider the intellect from the standpoint of its activity but only insofar as it is the recipient of the intellective act. However, they do not tell us that the intellect is not active at all. The argument from authority cannot be used negatively [i.e., for what it does not say]." *Op. Oxon.,* I, d. 3, q. 7, n. 37.

[73] *Ibid.*

If the human intellect is an active power, insist the upholders
of the opposite theory, how shall we account for the fact that
we know it only through its acts, that is, only after we come
to know other things? More specifically, we do not know anything that is not in act. Hence the fact that it is not possible
for us to know our own intellect except insofar as it has been
actuated by the knowledge of some other reality outside the
soul seems to confirm the opinion that our faculty is pure
potentiality in the order of intelligibility *(in genere intelligibilium),* just as primary matter is in the order of bodily
things *(in genere corporalium).*

The intellect, answers Scotus, exists as an intellect, agent or
possible, even before it knows anything. It is *in actu primo,*
that is to say, it has its actuality as intellective power even
before it acquires any knowledge, and is therefore knowable
by its very nature. The fact that we do not know it directly
but only indirectly through its acts *(in actu secundo* and not
in actu primo) does not depend on its nature as pure potentiality, but solely on the law that governs human knowledge.
According to this law, human knowledge always takes its
lead from the phantasm.[74]

It will be readily seen that this doctrine is the natural outcome of Duns Scotus' notion of potency, a notion different
from that of St. Thomas. If the human intellect is a knowing
power, it must, according to Scotus, possess its own essential
actuality whereby it exists as a power capable of all possible
intellections. Hence the intellect's indetermination must not
be understood as though the intellect had no act whatsoever,
but only as an indetermination of activity. In other words, the

---

[74] *Ibid.,* n. 38: "The statement that the intellect is not something intelligible before it is actuated in the act of knowing, must not be understood in the sense that our intellective faculty is pure potency, but
rather in the sense that before knowing an object the intellect cannot
be grasped directly. This is due to the fact that in the present state
human knowledge is only possible through sensible experience."

intellect is indeterminate (i.e., it is capable of knowing all things) not because it is pure passivity, but because it is an unlimited activity. Pure passivity is, as it were, unlimited poverty; unlimited activity is, on the contrary, boundless wealth. What is indeterminate in the first way cannot act without being actuated by some form which, by communicating to it a nature, communicates to it a principle, a capacity for actions. What is indeterminate in the second way does not need a form that communicates to it the activity in order to act, but only the presence of an object which serves as a terminus, and offers a necessary point of reference and application for the unlimited energy of the spirit.[75] Briefly, the object does not perfect our faculty by making it active, but only by determining it, through its presence, to know something in the concrete.

At this point a question may arise. If the human intellect is active by its nature, how is it that without the concurrence of the object it cannot know, that is, it is incapable of producing by itself concrete acts of knowledge? How can an activity be understood without acts? Duns Scotus solves this difficulty by pointing out that the activity of the human intellect is unlimited but not infinite. It is unlimited in the sense that the intellect has *being as being* as its proper and adequate object, and is by its nature ordained to understand the whole being. However, not being an infinite intellect, it does not have within itself the whole being, and must seek outside itself, i.e., in things, in other beings, the necessary integration of its own power. Only an infinite thought is by nature perfectly in act, for only in this case thought and being, subject and object, are united in a perfect and infinite unity. "The perfection of the intellect combined with its imperfection gives rise to an insufficient activity. It would be a sufficient activity capable of knowing all objects, only if it had within itself

[75] *Ibid.*, n. 30.

the whole of being." [76] Thus human knowledge finds its sufficient cause only in the natural and necessary union of the activity of the soul with the object. Yet the object does not act on the soul in any way; its collaboration consists simply in being present to the soul as the terminus of its intellective activity.

It is commonly understood that to be the object of a faculty means principally that the thing impresses its own species on the faculty. This, affirms Duns Scotus, is an erroneous conception. A thing is in effect the object of a faculty mainly because this latter tends toward it as the terminus of its activity. [77] Hence the intellective act is not the result of a reciprocal action of the object on the soul and vice versa, but simply of a causal collaboration between them. It is a natural and necessary collaboration that finds its explanation and foundation in the fact that thought is by its nature ordained to being, just as being is ordained to thought in which it is revealed. What makes the presence of the object to the soul fecund and efficacious is precisely this reciprocal tie existing between being and thought, and similarly, between being and will. Because knowledge is this fecund meeting of intellect (subject) and object, in order to explain it we must admit that both intellect and object participate actively in its production. The meeting of intellect and object is, in other words, a reciprocal impulse of one toward the other.

Duns Scotus places his solution under the patronage of St. Augustine, who in *De Trinitate,* book IX, writes as follows: "It is clear that everything we know concurs in the production

---

[76] *Ibid.,* n. 26.

[77] *Metaph.,* VII, q. 18, n. 11: "I reply that the first statement is false, for it belongs to the intellective power not only to receive the species of the object but also to tend with its act toward the object. This second attribute is more essential to the power than the first one. . . . The object is an object more because the power tends toward it, than because it impresses upon the power its own species."

of its idea. Indeed, knowledge is the product of both the knower and the thing known." [78] This is a most important statement. It shows that Duns Scotus, too, was aware that his gnoseology was more in line with Augustinian thought than with Aristotelian philosophy. It shows also his conviction that human knowledge is neither entirely a priori nor entirely a posteriori, but rather the synthesis of both.

---

[78] *Op. Oxon.,* I, d. 3, q. 7, n. 20. [St. Augustine's text referred to by Duns Scotus is from *De Trinitate,* lib. IX, chap. 12, n. 18; PL vol. 42, col. 970: "Unde liquido tenendum est quod omnis res quamcumque cognoscimus, congenerat in nobis notitiam sui. Ab utroque enim notitia paritur, a cognoscente et cognito." *(Tr.)*]

V

EPISTEMOLOGICAL PROBLEMS

MAN BY nature desires to know. He desires to acquire not merely knowledge in general, but systematic knowledge of reality so as to embrace it in all its complexity and variety. To attain this organization and unification of the knowledge he acquires by his contact with external reality, man follows the lead of certain principles and laws of thought that are the very life and light of his intelligence. Man does not receive knowledge, nor does he create it; he constructs it. Knowledge is an intimate and vital exchange between subject and object, the unique and indivisible product of the meeting of soul and external reality.

THE VALUE OF KNOWLEDGE

A philosophical inquiry into knowledge gives rise to two main problems. The first refers to ideas, which are, as it were, the constructive material of science; the second concerns those principles and laws of thought which we may compare to the architectural plans of a building to be constructed. As regards ideas, the philosopher inquires about their relationship to things and to what extent they make things known to us; as regards principles and ideal laws, he asks himself whether they are merely principles and laws of thought or also principles and laws of being. Basically, we are confronted here with two aspects of one and the same problem, namely, the problem of the value of human knowledge. Does knowledge represent reality as it is in itself, or does it represent it only as I think it to be? In other words, is knowledge objective or is it merely subjective?

Like all medieval philosophers, Duns Scotus does not have an exact notion of the so-called critical problem, even though that problem, as stated by modern philosophy, is a pseudo-problem.[79] He is convinced that thought has an intentional character as well as an essential relationship to being. Indeed, this is the only correct way to understand thought. Those who think otherwise do not really know what thinking means. Yet it cannot be denied that by his doctrine of *ens in-quantum ens* as the proper object of the human intellect, the Subtle Doctor emphasizes the intentionality of our knowledge and gives an explicit demonstration of it. The essential objectivity of thought, and hence of human thought too, which in this respect does not differ from any other thought, must certainly not be understood in a näive or naturalistic way, as though the idea were so perfectly adequate to the thing that both would have exactly the same characteristics. By definition, ideal being is not real being. No wonder then that the idea has a character different from that of the concrete thing, and vice versa. The explanation of this fact can be found in the Scotistic doctrine of knowledge expounded in the preceding chapter.

Knowledge, Duns Scotus teaches us, arises from the causal concurrence of the soul and the object; it is an effect of two

---

[79] In this connection I might refer to the thesis that Prof. Gustavo Bontadini of the University of the Sacred Heart, Milan, has been defending and proving these past years, namely, that a gnoseological presupposition lies at the root of modern philosophy.

causes and does not depend either on the soul or on the thing alone. This causal dependence implies a correspondence and an entitative similarity between the effect and its cause. When the effect depends on two partial efficient causes, it will not be entirely similar to either one or the other; it will only be partially similar to each of them. From this it follows that the effect will never be more perfect than the two partial causes taken together, but it will conceivably be more perfect than one cause taken separately. Likewise, if the two causes differ as to their perfection, the efficiency, and therefore the influence, of one will be greater than the efficiency and the influence of the other in the production of the effect. This, as we have seen, is precisely the case in knowledge.

The consequences are evident. First, the idea must be objective, for the thing known concurs effectively with the intellect to produce the idea, and thus manifests its own nature in it. On the other hand, the idea is not merely a photograph of the thing, for the intellect does not receive it passively. Rather, it produces it as a principal cause in cooperation with the object. Second, insofar as it depends on the object, the idea is always a *similitudo,* a revelation of the thing; insofar as it depends on the soul and is an act of it, it is not a mere material image of the thing, but a spiritual entity with its own proper mode of being, namely, universality. Third, inasmuch as it depends on the object and the soul together, the idea is not something that we know, but something that helps us to know. It is not, as scholastics used to say, an *objectum quod,* but an *objectum quo* of our intellect. It exists as an intentional entity, that is, as a necessary means of reference between thought and being, between intellect and thing.[80]

---

[80] Speaking of the relationship between the intellective act and the thing, Duns Scotus says that they are related to each other as the measurable and the measure, or measure and the measurable, depending on whether we consider the created intellect, which knows only in col-

This doctrine shows clearly that one cannot pass judgment on the objectivity of knowledge from the greater or lesser degree of conformity that exists between the object and its concept. Such a conformity is in direct relation to the subjective capacity of the knower to grasp the attributes contained in the object. The objectivity of our knowledge rests rather on the causal dependence of the intellective act upon the object and on the constant and necessary relation of likeness *per imitationem* between the thing and the idea that represents it.

Once the objectivity of human knowledge is understood in this way, the contrast between the characteristic attributes of the concept and those of the concrete thing no longer constitutes a difficulty; it will appear, on the contrary, to be the natural consequence of what has just been shown, namely, that the intellective act is an inseparable effect resulting from the two partial efficient causes that produce it and are different in nature and perfection. On the other hand, from the fact that man knows only through universal concepts, it will not be permissible to conclude that he directly knows only the universal, and that the individual is known only indirectly. This doctrine cannot be accepted by Duns Scotus for two reasons: first, because it goes against our own experience, and second, because it contradicts other doctrines of his system.[81] This will be seen in the next section.

INTUITIVE KNOWLEDGE OF THE SINGULAR

An individual is a being that is richer than its specific essence. *Haecceitas* is in effect the last perfection of a thing,

---

laboration with the object, or the divine intellect, which, in the act of knowing, produces the object *in esse intelligibili*. The relationships between object and will are analogous. For Scotus' exact notion of the way in which the object is the measure of the intellect cf. *Quodlibet*, q. 13, n. 12.

[81] *Metaph.*, VII, qq. 14 and 15; *De Anima*, q. 22.

a perfection that is necessary for a thing's concrete existence. Only the individual exists in the complete sense of the term. Hence if being is synonymous with intelligibility, the individual *secundum se* must be more intelligible than the species. Yet it must be recognized that in his present condition man is unable to grasp a thing's "haecceity," even though he knows things in their concrete existence, and therefore as individuals. This amounts to saying that man knows the individual but not singularity, understood as the precise reason that makes the individual characteristics inhere in a thing.[82] More specifically, he does not know the reason why these characteristics are the individuating notes of this particular thing rather than of another. Knowledge of the haecceity of all things would constitute full knowledge of all reality: an impossible task for our intellect in its present condition.

The thing existing here and now in its concreteness is known directly not only by the senses but also by the intellect, which grasps it by an intuitive knowledge. Intuitive knowledge is distinct from abstractive knowledge, which always prescinds from the existence of the object known. When considered in its phenomenological origin, human knowledge always starts from the intuition of the concrete thing. The product of this first meeting of intellect and thing is the *species specialissima,* or the idea of the individual thing. This idea is quite proper to the object that stands before me; it is through it that the intellect has the first grasp of what it wants to know. However, as soon as my intellect tries to find out exactly what the thing is and looks for its definition, it has recourse to universal concepts, precisely because it is incapable of grasping the haecceity. Through the *species specialissima* I know the object only in a confused manner ("a thing is known confusedly when only the meaning of its term is known"[83]). Once

---

[82] *Op. Oxon.,* IV, d. 45, q. 3, n. 21.
[83] *Ibid.,* I, d. 3, q. 2, n. 21.

I have grasped by means of the concepts of genus and species its exact place and meaning in the manifold of reality, then I know it distinctly, at least to the extent that my intellect can know it. "A thing is known distinctly," says Duns Scotus, "when I can give its definition." [84]

Thus Duns Scotus attributes to man intuitive knowledge along with abstractive and conceptual knowledge. It is by no means a perfect intuition, for it is only an initial and confused kind of knowledge; yet it is not thereby less important. For the human intellect it is the necessary starting point, its first way of getting in touch with reality. It is like a spiritual sense by which we intellectually perceive the reality that affects our senses and the modifications that take place in them.[85]

THE NATURE OF SCIENTIFIC KNOWLEDGE

In Duns Scotus' system not only sensations, but all the acts that constitute our interior life are grasped intuitively. The intuition of our interior acts is particularly important to him because it helps solve the problem of scientific knowledge, which is above all a problem of certitude and evidence.

According to Aristotle, four things are required for scientific knowledge: "It must be certain, that is, without error and doubt, of a necessary object, based on evidence, and attained by syllogistic reasoning. The definition of science given in the first book of the *Posterior Analytics* may be referred to." [86] To a superficial reader it may appear that Duns Scotus accepts the Aristotelian notion of science without question; but that is not the case. In fact, he calls our attention to the conse-

---

[84] *Ibid.*

[85] *Ibid.*, IV, d. 45, q. 3, n. 17: "The intellect knows not only the universals, but it knows also intuitively the objects known by the senses, for a superior and more perfect power knows all that an inferior power knows. It knows also the sensations."

[86] *Ibid.*, I, Prologus; qq. 3 and 4 lateralis, n. 26.

quences following from Aristotle's second requisite for science. If it is a characteristic of science, taken in the strict sense of the term, that its object be necessary, all contingent realities are *ipso facto* excluded from the field of scientific knowledge. This consequence could be easily admitted by Aristotle, who conceived the world as being ruled by necessity, but not by one who maintains that reality is the effect of a free creative act of God. Creationism bears with it the conviction that all things apart from God are contingent. Hence, either the concept of science must be modified, or one must deny the title to all sciences that are not strictly deductive. This is tantamount to saying that man cannot rise to true scientific knowledge. For if it is true that certain sciences, like metaphysics and mathematics, are predominantly deductive, they are not exclusively so.

Let us consider metaphysics as an example. Insofar as it claims to be a total vision of reality in its ultimate and supreme causes, metaphysics ought to be strictly deductive in character. From the definition of its object one should be able to draw a series of inferences that, starting from the most simple and universal causes or principles, will lead us to the ultimate effects that follow logically from them.[87] A purely deductive metaphysics, although entirely possible in itself, has never been taught by any philosopher since it is not practical for the human mind. "Because of the impotence of our intellect, we go from sensible things, which are less known in themselves, to the knowledge of immaterial things, which are in themselves more intelligible and constitute, as it were, the principles of knowledge. As such, they are known in a metaphysics that is different from ours."[88]

Accordingly, human knowledge, as a whole, must be but the mind's ascent from effects to cause, from contingent things

---

[87] *Metaph.*, Prologus, n. 9.
[88] *Ibid.*

to their reason. It is necessary insofar as it is the indispensable explanation of reality, but not in the sense that it necessarily produces its effects; it is necessary *in ascendendo,* but not *in descendendo.* The metaphysical necessity or lack of necessity of the object, remarks Duns Scotus, is a perfection that is in the object, not in the knowledge I have of it. My knowledge is necessary only when I cannot help having it and cannot lose it; it is not necessary merely because it is concerned with a necessary object. Hence science, whether necessary or not in the sense that has just been explained, is always science. What distinguishes it from mere opinion or simple knowledge is its certitude and evidence, not its necessity.[89]

EVIDENCE AS THE ULTIMATE MOTIVE OF CERTITUDE AND CRITERION OF TRUTH

Can man attain an absolutely certain and evident knowledge? It is a fact that man adheres to certain propositions with a firmness that defies any doubt. This is the case, first of all, with propositions or principles that are self-evident and with all the conclusions that can be drawn from them by syllogistic reasoning. The evidence of such propositions is sufficiently grounded in the terms that make them up. I cannot understand these terms without understanding at the same time the logical nexus binding them together. Thus, as soon as I formulate the concepts of the whole and the part, I see immediately that the whole is greater than the part. I cannot admit the possibility of being deceived, for it is impossible for me to think otherwise. Even if the senses, which furnish

---

[89] *Op. Oxon.,* Prologus; qq. 3 and 4 lateralis, n. 28: "I say here that it is of the perfection of science to be evident and certain. To be science of a necessary object is a circumstance that has to do with the object, not with science as such. For even though science may be concerned with a necessary object, it can in itself be contingent and be destroyed by oblivion."

me with the terms of comparison, were constantly deceiving me, the truth of such propositions would not change. The evidence of the nexus between subject and predicate does not have sensible experience as its cause, but springs out of the terms inasmuch as they are present to my mind. Sense experience does not cause my understanding; it simply offers to my mind an occasion of seeing the necessary tie binding the two terms together. Hence, the validity of such propositions rests entirely on the activity of my mind which compares the two concepts.

The same must be said of the evident validity of syllogistic reasoning. This, too, is due entirely to the light of my intellect. Once the premises and the inference are evident, the conclusion also is evident.[90]

On this premise, the strictly scientific character of the so-called deductive sciences is assured. Indeed, their principles and conclusions are endowed with the two constitutive properties of scientific knowledge, namely, evidence and certitude.

Let us examine the case of the inductive sciences, or those sciences which rest on sense experience. The procedure of these sciences is well known. From the observation of a certain number of similar facts, such as water boiling at 100 degrees centigrade, a general law is formulated that is valid for all cases of the same kind. On what precisely rests the certitude and evidence of scientific laws? What is their basis? There is no doubt that it cannot be experience alone. Experience assures me only that in all the observed cases, when a particular factor or circumstance is present (heating to 100°), a certain effect follows (the boiling of the water), but it can in no way assure me that this will always be so. There is no absolute necessity that water will boil exactly at 100°. Consequently, the bond that the general law establishes between the two terms is far from being evident. Empirical evidence is only

---

[90] *Ibid.*, I, d. 3, q. 4, nn. 7-8.

valid for the cases experienced. The evidence needed for the scientific value of the laws representing the conclusions drawn from experimental premises must therefore have its foundation outside experience.

For Duns Scotus the foundation of induction rests on this general principle: "Every phenomenon which has been repeatedly experienced, and which depends on a cause that is not free, is a natural effect of that cause." [91] That a cause which is not free always produces the effect to which it is naturally ordained is a self-evident proposition. Hence the constancy of the bond existing between two phenomena, as observed by experience, can be explained only by admitting that the first phenomenon produces the second, not by chance or arbitrarily, but because it is ordained to produce it by its very nature. Thus, legitimate use of the inductive method rests both on the evidence of an analytical proposition and on the evidence of my experience. Its scientific value is fully justified by the concurrence of this twofold evidence.[92]

As will be readily seen, Duns Scotus has clear and precise ideas on induction; he knows its meaning and acknowledges its value. Furthermore, in one of his *Quaestiones subtilissimae in Metaphysicam Aristotelis,*[93] where he discusses at length the legitimate use and value of scientific induction, he describes a concrete, particular way of proceeding in scientific research from which the two essential methods of induction can be derived, namely, the method of agreement and the method of difference.[94]

For Duns Scotus the objectivity of our concepts is thus assured by the fact that the thing concurs to produce them as a partial efficient cause, while the value of the proofs and

---

[91] *Ibid.,* n. 9.
[92] *Ibid.*
[93] *Metaph.,* I, q. 4.
[94] *Ibid.,* n. 17.

scientific conclusions rests on their evidence, whether immediate or mediate. Evidence is therefore for him the norm of certitude as well as the criterion of truth. Will the value of human knowledge be thereby guaranteed from all points of view? The sceptic may raise a further objection.

It is a fact that certain truths force themselves upon man because of their intrinsic evidence, so that it is impossible to reject them. However, if we take a closer look at the question, we will see that this does not as yet solve in an absolute, definite way the problem of the objective value of my knowledge. Who can assure me that at a particular moment I am reasoning correctly, that I truly see the truth, and that I am not dreaming? What proof do I have of the objective validity of my reasoning? May it not be that my reasoning is merely the product of a sick mind or the conclusions of a sleepwalker?

There is no other guarantee or assurance, answers Duns Scotus, than that of consciousness, which is simply the intuition of my own acts. Granted that during my dreams I can make the same acts of reason as when awake, I can nevertheless clearly distinguish between what I thought during my dreams and what I am thinking when awake. Briefly, my acts and the normal functioning of my intellective power are known to me intuitively, and no objection whatsoever can be raised against this intuitive evidence and certitude. To one who still insists and asks for an extrinsic criterion in order to judge whether in my act of thinking and reasoning I am really awake, the only answer that can be given is this: "You are not convinced because you are stubborn." [95] That is to say, your doubt has no foundation except in your obstinacy in doubt. When my intellective faculty "is functioning properly and when it is not, is something self-evident; otherwise nothing could be known for certain. When confronted with an evident proposition, I could always ask myself whether it is in a state

---

[95] *Op. Oxon.*, I, d. 3, q. 4, n. 15.

of wakefulness or in a state of sleep that that appears to me as evident." [96] To doubt the value of this intuitive evidence is to make all affirmation and all reasoning impossible; it is a doubt from which there is no way out. The very impossibility of this reveals its inconsistency and absurdity.

CONCLUDING REMARKS

The preceding statements are of utmost importance. They are not only philosophically sound, but they also show the importance the Subtle Doctor attributes to the intuitive knowledge of our internal acts. Intuitive knowledge possesses evidence equal to that of first principles,[97] and offers in addition what may be called basic evidence; for it is upon it that rest, in ultimate analysis, all other evidences. Were this evidence lacking to us, the whole edifice of human knowledge could rightly be called fiction. Thus we see once more how deeply Scotus' thought has been influenced by the philosophy of St. Augustine. It is certainly not from Aristotle that Duns Scotus learned to appreciate intuitive knowledge in general and to attribute to the intuition of our acts in particular the importance we have just considered in the foregoing section. The setting, the problems, the formulas may well be Aristotelian in tone, but the doctrine is of truly Augustinian origin. If Duns Scotus has adopted many elements from Aristotle, he has skillfully merged and integrated them with the teachings of St. Augustine.

A further important observation must be made by way of conclusion to the present chapter. For Duns Scotus human science is possible only as a synthesis of induction and deduction. Deductive sciences begin with sensible experience and stand firm upon it as upon solid ground; inductive sciences,

---

[96] *Ibid.*
[97] *Ibid.*, n. 10.

in turn, receive their strength from the value of an analytical
proposition which itself is at the very basis of induction. Thus
we find in science a new application, a new development of
the law of partial efficient causes. Not only are individual intellective acts the result of the causal concurrence of the object
and the soul, but science as well results from it. Here sensible
experience takes the place of the object, while the principles
represent the part of the intellect. The former offers the terms
and the facts, that is, the material to be organized, while the
intellect by means of its principles gives the dynamic pattern
according to which the unification is to be carried out. In
so doing, the intellect makes unification possible and directs
it to the summit of its perfection.

At this point the question arises spontaneously: where do
these ideal laws come from? How do you explain their presence
in the intellect? Duns Scotus tells us explicitly that they are
not derived from experience. Experience offers only the occasion for their manifestation and for their activation. "As regards this knowledge [of principles], sense does not act as
a cause with the intellect, but only as an occasion." [98] It is not
difficult to complete Scotus' thought. This can be done by recalling once more his doctrine of the proper object of the
human intellect. In virtue of its natural ordination to being,
the whole of being, human intelligence has in itself an exigency
for, as well as a guide toward, total truth. This explains why
our intellect is not closed within the limits of experience and
does not let itself be dominated by it; on the contrary, it rules
over it and directs it in accordance with the laws of being. We
are then justified in saying, rather, we must say, that through
the sciences man tends to the unification of reality. For the
concept of being in which man knows all other things and
which he somehow already has within himself (virtual in-

---

[98] *Ibid.,* n. 8.

natism)* predisposes his intellect to unity by communicating to it the exigency and power for its attainment.

Here again we are bound to admit that for Duns Scotus, as for the Augustinian school, a man knows things not because they force themselves upon his intellect, but because his intellect seeks them, and therefore, in a certain sense, it already knows them. Experience is a kind of nourishment for a man's intellect. Yet, just as nourishment is of no value to one that does not possess actual life, so this kind of intellectual nourishment would be useless if the intellect were not in act before its contact with experience. This constitutive act of the human intellect is precisely its intrinsic determination to being, or, should I say, its natural craving for being. Herein lies the root of all a priori elements in human knowledge.

---

* Concerning this so-called "virtual innatism" of the idea of being, see my observation above after n. 11.

VI

INFINITE BEING

THE CONCEPT OF INFINITE BEING

BEING *qua* being, that is, being understood in its pure formality whereby it is predicated of everything that exists in some manner, is neither necessarily finite nor infinite. Finitude and infinity do not enter into the concept of being, nor are they its transcendental attributes.[99] Accordingly, we can think of being either as finite or as infinite.

That finite being actually exists is a fact of experience. Does the infinite being also exist? This is not a truth of immediate evidence to us, nor is it a truth that forces itself upon us by the simple enunciation of its terms. A priori, we can only know the noncontradiction or nonimpossibility of an infinite

---

[99] *Op. Oxon.*, I, d. 2, q. 2, n. 31. [Gilson's observation in this respect is worth quoting: "The being that is thought as common to God and creatures is, by definition, the being neither of God nor creatures. And *that, by the way, is why the Scotist proofs of God's existence are really proofs;* the very fact that they start from being supposes that this concept is not the concept of God; for were it so there would be nothing to prove, we should have no need to look further. Univocity no more

132

being. At the most, we can show, on the basis of certain considerations, the fittingness of its existence. Further than that we cannot go.

Let us start with the notion of infinity. It is not impossible to think of a quantitative magnitude made up of an infinity of successive parts. In the supposition that these parts do not exist successively but simultaneously—which is a greater perfection—there will be an infinite being in act.

On the other hand, an infinite activity is more perfect than a quantitative infinity. But what is more perfect is also more possible. Hence, if a quantitative infinity is possible, an infinite activity has an even greater degree of possibility.

Moreover, if an infinite being were something contradictory, my intellect, whose proper object is being, would immediately notice the contrast between the concept of being and the concept of infinite, just as my sense of hearing immediately notices contrasts in sound. Hence it is not without meaning that my intellect can think without any difficulty of an infinite being. Far from experiencing any difficulty, it enjoys a certain delight in this, as though it were confronted with the most perfect metaphysical agreement in which the plenitude of intelligibility corresponds with the plenitude of being.[100]

ST. ANSELM'S ONTOLOGICAL ARGUMENT FOR THE EXISTENCE OF GOD

On the basis of the foregoing considerations, Duns Scotus proposes a new interpretation of St. Anselm's famous onto-

---

provides a starting point for the beatific vision than analogy, for the dividing line between man and God is situated on another plane; it results from the fact of creation." *The Spirit of Mediaeval Philosophy*, *op. cit.*, p. 265. (Italics are the Translator's.) *(Tr.)*]

[100] *Ibid.*, n. 32.

logical argument.[101] To say that God is "that than which
nothing greater can be thought of," is equivalent to saying that
God is an infinite being. Hence what has been said above in
regard to the composite concept of "infinite being" is also valid
for the Anselmian definition taken in its broadest sense. "A
being than which nothing greater can be thought of" is not in
itself contradictory, any more than is an infinite being.

This is an important point that deserves to be emphasized, for
it is precisely upon the principle of noncontradiction that the
whole strength of the argument rests. St. Anselm's argument
must then be understood in the following way. "God is such a
being that, if possible to be conceived without contradiction, no
greater being can be conceived without contradiction." [102] In
fact, if God is the being "than which nothing greater can be
conceived," and if such a being implies no contradiction, God is
possible. But if possible, He must also exist in reality.

The evidence for this conclusion will appear from the following reflections. If God were merely possible, He would exist
only in my mind and not in reality. Consequently, He would
not be God, namely, the "being than which nothing greater can
be thought of." For a real being is more perfect than a possible
being, since this latter cannot be realized, i.e., brought into
existence, except by a being that already exists. Thus, if God
were merely possible, He would depend on another being: He
would no longer be God. This is tantamount to saying that God
would at the same time be possible and not possible, which is

---

[101] *Ibid.* [This is the argument for the existence of God proposed by
St. Anselm (1033-1109) in his *Proslogium.* The argument goes from
the idea of God as a being than which nothing greater can be thought
of to God's existence. In scholastic terminology it is called an argument
a priori or *a simultaneo,* while the specific term for it is the *ratio
Anselmi.* Immanuel Kant called it less properly "the ontological
argument." *(Tr.)*]

[102] *Ibid.*

an evident contradiction. By definition, God cannot depend on other beings. Therefore He is not possible except as a being independent of any other being, i.e., as a self-existing being. Once His possibility is established, His actual existence is thereby also established.

What value does Duns Scotus attribute to his "coloration" of the Anselmian argument? Interpreters are not of one accord on this point. Some consider it to be the Subtle Doctor's complete adherence to the argument of St. Anselm; others claim to see in it the real Scotistic demonstration of God's existence; a third group is of the opinion that Duns Scotus' coloration of the Anselmian argument has nothing to do with the Scotistic demonstration of God's existence, but is merely one of the arguments with which he proves God's infinity.

The purpose of this study does not allow me to go into a detailed discussion, and I will summarize my opinion in a few brief observations. The Scotistic coloration can be reduced to the following hypothetic syllogism: If God (*ens infinitum, ens quo maius cogitari non potest*) is possible, He exists. But God is possible. Therefore, He exists. The value of the conclusion rests on the solidity of the premises. St. Anselm's main preoccupation has been to point out the solidity of the major, thus neglecting the minor, which appears as a statement without foundation. Further, one cannot only challenge St. Anselm for the evident weakness of the minor, but he can also call in question the solidity of the major itself, namely, the right to conclude from the possibility of God to His existence. However, there is no difficulty here for Duns Scotus, since he accepts the major premise. The transition from God's possibility to His existence seems to him to be beyond question. His coloration tends mainly to establish the value of the minor, namely, that God is possible. How does the Subtle Doctor proceed in his argumentation?

We have already seen that by a demonstration a priori we cannot arrive beyond a mere probability. "It does not seem that the minor of this syllogism [that infinity is not repugnant to being] can be demonstrated a priori."[103] Why? A truth is demonstrated a priori when one attains it by the simple explanation of the meaning of the terms involved. Now if we attempt to analyze the concept of the term that acts as a subject, *being,* and the concept of the term that acts as a predicate, *infinite,* we see immediately that such an analysis is impossible. For, on the one hand, the concept of being is a most simple concept that cannot be reduced to any other concept; on the other hand, our notion of the infinite is an indirect notion which is related to the notion of the finite. "The infinite is that which transcends a finite being not according to any definite proposition, but beyond any limit we can think of."[104] Since we understand the infinite through the finite, we cannot grasp the intimate relation existing between infinity and being, nor can we grasp the logical tie that binds the predicate to the subject. We can only come to understand this, namely, that an infinite being is not an absurdity, and that our intellect considers it with ever-increasing delight. In other words, all we understand is that we cannot discard a priori the possibility that an infinite being exists.

From this it will be readily seen that for Duns Scotus the *ratio Anselmi* cannot have an apodictic value. It is simply a *persuasio* like the other considerations that precede it. To make it clear that to think of the existence of an infinite being is not absurd, and that the intellect has a certain tendency to admit the existence of such a being, is not enough to conclude that the infinite being actually exists. Duns Scotus himself seems to be of this opinion when he writes that the possibility of an infinite being "does not seem to be demonstrable a priori ..., however, here are some persuasive considerations...."[105]

---

[103] *Ibid.,* n. 31.
[104] *Ibid.*
[105] *Ibid.*

THE A POSTERIORI PROOFS FOR THE EXISTENCE OF GOD

Before positing the problem of the existence of an infinite being, it was necessary to see whether it was not perhaps a pseudo-problem. It would have been such if the proposition, "A being is infinite," were self-evident, as is the proposition, "The whole is greater than the part," and also in the case that the concept of an infinite being would have been proved to be a contradictory concept. On the other hand, it must be admitted that from the simple nonimpossibility of a thing one cannot at once infer its existence. From *esse* to *posse* the transition is valid, but from simple *posse* to *esse* the inference is not licit.[106]

To demonstrate on a sure basis the existence of God, Duns Scotus believes a twofold procedure is possible. Starting from the observation that things of our experience are changing realities, and that what changes and becomes does not have in itself the sufficient reason for its operations and for its existence, the first approach makes it clear that only the existence of a being which is not subject to change or becoming can justify the existence of the beings that become. This is substantially the process that St. Thomas developed along strictly philosophical lines in his first three ways.

Akin to this approach is another, which has its starting point in the possibility of things. The existence of things that come into being is a fact of immediate, sensible evidence, but the possibility that such things exist, like myself who am writing, the house that shelters me, the sun which at this moment breaks through an autumn day, is a necessary truth that forces itself upon my mind. If, by supposition, the whole world that surrounds me were to plunge into nothingness, or to reveal itself

---

[106] *De Primo Principio*, chap. III, n. 1: ". . . for those things which are conceded about an actual being can also be conceded about a possible being, but not conversely."

as nothing but a dream-world, it would still be true that such a world can exist, that it can be created. Here again I am compelled to ask myself whether this possibility has its foundation in the things themselves, or in another being with a different nature.

Even though Duns Scotus does not find any fault in the former process, which he admits as being perfectly valid and sound, nevertheless he prefers this latter process. Let us examine, within the limits imposed by the nature of this study, the way followed by the Subtle Doctor in establishing the truth of God's existence.*

---

* Concerning Duns Scotus' proofs of God's existence, Allan B. Wolter writes in the introduction to his study, "Duns Scotus and the Existence and Nature of God," *Proceedings of the American Catholic Philosophical Association,* XXVIII (1954), 94-95: "Of the great scholastics, perhaps no one devoted more attention and care to developing a proof for the existence of God than did Duns Scotus. Unlike Aquinas, Bonaventure, Henry of Ghent and so many others, he made no attempt to exploit the multitude of ways he considered possible, but rather concentrated his efforts on a single proof incorporating into it what he believed to be the best elements of the arguments of his predecessors and contemporaries. From the time when he presented the first draft of his proof as a bachelor of theology at Oxford to the day some eight years later when death found him still busy revising his major works for publication, the Subtle Scot had reworked his proof no less than three times that we know of. The changes, aimed principally at economy of thought and greater logical systematization, left the major outlines of the argument unaltered."

It is no doubt the highly convincing character of Duns Scotus' proof for God's existence that led Thomas Merton to affirm: "It is getting to be rather generally admitted that, for accuracy and depth and scope, this [Duns Scotus'] is the most perfect and complete and thorough proof for the existence of God that has ever been worked out by any man." *The Seven Storey Mountain* (New York: Harcourt, Brace and Co., 1948), p. 94. *(Tr.)*

The First Efficient Cause. "Some being is producible"
(*aliquod ens est effectibile*).[107] It is an undeniable, necessary
truth that some being, e.g., a man, a house or the sun, although
not necessarily existing, can by its very nature be produced or
brought into existence. If the intrinsic (logical) foundation of
this possibility is in the nature of the thing, its extrinsic (real)
foundation must be found either in itself, in nothing, or in another being. It cannot be nothing, for nothing cannot be the
cause of anything. To say that nothing is the cause of something is equivalent to saying that the thing in question has no
cause; it would amount to solving the problem by denying it.
The extrinsic foundation cannot be the thing itself, for it is
impossible that a being give existence to itself: "Nothing can
produce or give existence to itself."[108] To give existence to
itself a being would have to exist—for how could it act without existing?—and not exist—for how could it receive existence
if it were already existing?—at one and the same time, which
is a contradiction. We must, therefore, look for the real foundation of the extrinsic possibility of a thing in a being distinct
from the producible being.

This being, in turn, either exists and acts in its own right, or
in virtue of another being. In the first hypothesis, we are confronted with a being that is possible by itself, that by its nature
can only produce but not be produced, or, to use Scotus' terminology, that is *effectivum* but not *effectibile*. If the second
hypothesis is correct, that is, if the being in question is *effectivum* but only insofar as it is itself in turn *effectible* or receives
existence and activity from another, then we must go on and
look for a third being that is the foundation of the possibility
of the first and the second. This process will continue until we
meet what we are seeking, namely, a being that has in itself
the reason for its own possibility and for the possibility of all

---

[107] *Op. Oxon.*, I, d. 2, q. 2, n. 11.
[108] *Ibid.*

other beings. This search cannot go on forever, or else we would have to renounce finding the reason for the effectibility that was our starting point. We would have to say that there are beings which are possible, because producible, and not possible, because they would lack the real foundation of their possibility. This is evidently absurd.

We can therefore conclude that nothing would be possible if there did not exist a being which has the power to produce other beings, without itself being produced, a being that by its very nature has an autonomous, unparticipated activity which is the source of all perfections. But that certain things are possible is, as previously seen, a necessary truth. Hence by the same token we must affirm that this first being is, in the most absolute sense of the term, necessarily possible.

The question may be asked: is not a primary and absolutely independent activity a contradiction, an absurdity? Duns Scotus anticipates this objection and has his answer prepared. Activity is a simple perfection which does not necessarily include an imperfection, as does, for example, the power of reasoning. Consequently, an activity which in every respect is most perfect cannot be considered an impossibility. The more an agent depends on other things in its activity, the more imperfect it is; and, on the contrary, the more its autonomy of operation increases, the greater is its perfection. Therefore, if a most perfect activity is not a contradiction, neither is an agent that is pure act, nor an agent that is the efficient cause of all things without itself depending on any other efficient cause.[109]

Thus far two conclusions have been reached. First, in order to explain how some being can be produced, we have been compelled to admit the possibility of a being that produces without in turn being produced, that is, the possibility of a most perfect efficient cause. Second, we have proved that this most perfect efficient cause does not involve a contradiction,

---

[109] *Ibid.*, n. 14.

and therefore is not impossible. In other words, we have established the possibility of this most perfect efficient cause both positively and negatively.

Let us proceed further. This efficient cause, the first in an absolute sense, not only cannot depend on another efficient cause, but is also uncaused as far as other causes are concerned. In fact, if it cannot have an efficient cause, it follows *ipso facto* that neither does it depend on a final cause. The final cause is the motive impelling the efficient cause to act. Having no efficient cause, it cannot have a final cause; nor will it depend, as will be readily understood, on material and formal causes. Material and formal causes are the intrinsic causes of reality, inasmuch as reality is constituted by their meeting in a substantial union. However, this meeting, the synthesis of material cause with formal cause, cannot take place by itself; it must depend on the action of an efficient cause, which brings the two together precisely in order to constitute the new reality for a predetermined end. Hence, a being that does not depend on the extrinsic causes (efficient and final) is even more independent as to its intrinsic causes. The *primum effectivum* is thus also necessarily uncaused. It is precisely this incausability of the first efficient cause, whose possibility has thus far been established, that will permit us to demonstrate its existence in act.

If the *primum effectivum* which is possible *ex se* did not exist, we would be faced with the following three alternatives: either (1) we admit that a thing can be the cause of itself; or (2) that it is not truly *primum* and depends on another being; or (3) we must say that it is impossible. The first alternative is absurd; the other two are excluded on the basis of the preceding considerations. Hence the possibility of the *primum effectivum* cannot be conceived unless we admit its real existence. Stated otherwise, if the first cause does not exist, it is causable, since it is possible. But the first cause is by its nature incausable. Therefore, it is impossible to deny its existence. To do so

would amount to attributing to it two contradictory predicates by saying that it is incausable and causable at one and the
same time. Briefly, since we are compelled to admit the possibility of a first cause, we must likewise admit its existence.
To quote Scotus: "The first efficient cause in an absolute sense
can exist by itself; therefore, *it exists* by itself."[110]

The Supreme Final Cause. The same procedure and the same
considerations that have led us to affirm the existence of a
supreme efficient cause will also lead us to affirm the existence
of a supreme final cause and of a supremely perfect being. From
the very fact that a thing is producible and dependent on an
efficient cause, it must also be inferred that it depends on a
final cause. If it is true that something may be the result of
chance, it is likewise true that chance cannot be the starting
point of any causal order. To assert that everything happens by
chance, is to block the way to the search for the reason of
things; it is tantamount to denying the very intelligibility of
being.

Hence, to say that every effect must have a cause which is
directed to its production is merely another way of stating that
every possible thing has a final cause.[111] Therefore it is true
that "something is capable of being ordered to an end because
it is producible."[112] Just as in the order of efficient causes, so
also in the order of final causes, an infinite regress is impossible.
The demonstration of this principle as applied to the order of
efficient causes is equally valid when applied to the order of
final causes. Hence the conclusion must be drawn that *aliquid
finitivum est primum,* namely, that a supreme final cause is
possible. Since, on the other hand, to be truly supreme a final

---

[110] *Ibid.,* n. 16.
[111] *Ibid.,* n. 17.
[112] *De Primo Principio,* chap. II, n. 2.

cause must, like the *effectivum primum*, be incausable, it follows naturally that the *finitivum primum*, if possible, must exist.

The Most Perfect Being. The end to which a thing is ordered is the measure of its perfection. This means that the higher the end to which a being is destined, the more perfect is the being. Whereas the hierarchy of ends determines the hierarchy of perfections, the order of finality establishes the order of eminence. Hence the first being in the order of finality will also be the first being in the order of perfection; it will be a most perfect being. It will also be incausable. Being unable to have a superior end, it can have no efficient cause, and hence no cause at all. Thus the transition from possibility to existence, which has been proved valid in the case of a *primum effectivum* and a *primum finitivum*, is also valid in the case of a most perfect being.[113]

Scotus' Proofs vs. St. Thomas' Five Ways. By his threefold demonstration Duns Scotus is able to establish the existence of a being that is the supreme efficient cause, the supreme final cause, and supreme perfection. If we now compare the three Scotistic ways with St. Thomas' five ways, the following observations are in order.

(1) While St. Thomas' five ways are independent of one another, so that each one can be considered as an argument in its own right, Duns Scotus' three ways are like three flights of the same stairway, but in such a way that the second and the third flight can in turn occupy the place of the first.

(2) The logical elements of which the Scotistic ways are composed, are, as in St. Thomas' first three ways: a starting point; two principles—first, *"non est possibile quod aliquid sit*

---

[113] *Op. Oxon.,* I, d. 2, q. 2, n. 18.

causa efficiens sui ipsius," and second, *"infinitas est impossibilis in ascendendo"*;[114] and a conclusion. But while Scotus' two principles are substantially the same as those of St. Thomas, the starting point, the consequence, and the conclusion are different. St. Thomas starts with a fact and arrives at a fact; Duns Scotus starts with a possibility and arrives at a possibility. The transition from possibility to existence is made by a process unknown to the Aristotelian mentality. This process, as we pointed out when dealing with the Scotistic coloration, reminds us of the logical process of the Anselmian argument. Herein to a great extent lies the originality of the Scotistic demonstration, namely, in being a synthesis of St. Thomas and St. Anselm.

The weak point in St. Anselm's argument is his insufficient demonstration of the minor: God is possible. The most one can do by an a priori inquiry is to show that the existence of a most perfect being is neither impossible nor absurd. Perhaps one can go a little further and show that it is fitting that such a being exist. However, this will never suffice to give to the minor the kind of necessity an apodictic syllogism demands. What is not possible *a priori,* Duns Scotus makes possible *a posteriori.* By using the logical process of St. Thomas' ways based on the principle of causality, and by taking as his starting point the essence of things which reveals itself as necessarily possible, rather than their existence, he is able to demonstrate that the possibility of things also necessarily involves the possibility of the first and most perfect cause, God. When the minor premise has been thus strengthened and substantiated, the Anselmian argumentation attains in Duns Scotus its full demonstrative value.

It is not our purpose to discuss here the efficacy of Scotus' rescue of the famous ontological argument. Yet it will not be

---

[114] *Ibid.,* n. 11.

out of place to point out the ingenuity of his speculation, which infuses new life into the Augustinian inheritance which seemed to have been completely destroyed by Aristotelian attacks.

(3) Another point of difference between the Thomistic and the Scotistic demonstration is this: Duns Scotus is not convinced that he has successfully demonstrated the existence of God until he has also demonstrated the existence of an infinite being. We shall therefore resume our account and follow the last developments of the Scotistic ascent to God.

The Unicity of the First Cause. The first step in proving the existence of an infinite being is to demonstrate that the first efficient cause is also the first final cause and the most perfect being. This will not be a difficult task.

One who acts in virtue of his own nature does not act casually but for an end; and one who acts in virtue of his own nature antecedently to another agent acts also for an end superior to that of the other agent. Consequently, the first agent in an absolute order acts for the first end in an absolute order.

Further, the *primum effectivum* cannot depend on a final cause distinct from itself. Accordingly, the end of its acting must also be itself. Thus, besides being the first efficient cause, the *primum effectivum* is also the first final cause.

Again, inasmuch as none of the things produced, either mediately or immediately, by the first cause can equal this same cause in perfection—for the simple reason that each of those things is produced and depends on that cause—it follows that the first cause is also more perfect than all the things produced. This is equivalent to saying that the first cause is supremely eminent, that is, the most perfect existing being.

This opens the way to a demonstration of the unicity of God. The being that is first in the order of efficiency, in the order of finality, and in the order of perfection, is incausable, exists in its own right, and therefore exists by virtue of an intrinsic necessity (*est ex se necesse esse*).[115] Because of its nature, this being cannot admit anything that contradicts its own existence and perfection.

Let us suppose for a moment that two uncaused and necessary beings exist at the same time. Evidently they will have to possess, along with the common nature of necessary beings, certain characteristics that will distinguish one from the other. Two hypotheses are then possible. Either these distinctive characteristics demand by themselves the necessary existence of the being in which they are found, or they do not. If they do demand it, it means that such beings exist necessarily in virtue of two natural forms, one being shared in common and the other being proper to each one individually. But this is impossible, for every being is what it is in virtue of one nature alone, whereas these beings would be necessary in virtue of two natures. If they do not demand it, we would have the absurdity of a being which is partially necessary and partially not necessary.

The impossibility of the existence of two necessary beings is also manifest from the consideration that there would exist in such a case two ultimate ends of things, one independent of the other. Things would thus be ordered partly to the first end and partly to the second, with the result that they would be split and torn apart within themselves. They would be divided between two universes. Thus logic agrees perfectly with experience, which bears an ever-increasing witness to the harmonious unity of the universe, in proclaiming the unicity of the first cause.

INTELLECT AND WILL IN GOD

Having studied the first cause in its relation to the world, it is now time to study it in itself. The first truth that forces

---

[115] *Op. Oxon.,* I, d. 2, q. 2, n. 19.

itself upon our mind in this new approach is this: the first cause understands and wills. The order observed in the universe can be adequately explained only by admitting that all things act not merely by chance, but according to an internal disposition that determines them to act one way rather than another. This is another way of saying that the universe is ordered because it is endowed with finality.

If this is true of the universe, it must be much truer of the first cause, whose actions can in no way be left to the mercy of chance. As previously stated, the first cause cannot operate except on the basis of perfect independence and exclusively in virtue of its own nature. Hence the first cause must also act in an orderly way, that is, for an end.

Along with order, we observe that the universe is ruled by necessity. Many beings act according to order without being aware of it. Strictly speaking, as far as they are concerned, they would act even without an end in sight. Yet, since their actions tend toward an end, they must act in dependence on a first cause which loves their end in them and for them. It is a freely chosen and freely loved end. If it were otherwise, that is, if the first cause tended by necessity toward this end, then the cause would be controlled by the end. Such a supposition must be rejected, for it destroys the independence essential to the first cause.

Thus the first Maker understands and loves. Furthermore, in Him intellect and will are one and the same as His essence. This is also demanded by His perfection. We must briefly consider this point.

Knowledge and love of the first end moves the first cause to act; but the first final cause, as we have seen, is to be identified with the first efficient cause. Hence God acts inasmuch as He knows Himself and loves Himself. Now, the act by which God loves Himself as an end cannot be caused. Indeed, it could be caused only by the divine will. But why should the divine will tend to God, except because it knows and loves

Him? Thus an act of love would depend on another act of love; God would love Himself because He loves Himself, and so on to infinity, which is contradictory and meaningless. Consequently, the love God has for Himself inasmuch as He is the final cause of His own activity must be an absolute *first* as is His own activity. To say *first* in an absolute sense and to say incausable are one and the same thing.

On the other hand, that which is incausable is necessary, and, since only God is the necessary being *ex se,* it follows that the act by which the first cause knows and loves itself as an end is to be identified with the cause itself.

Again, by that same act by which God knows and loves Himself, He knows and loves all possible things. Actually the first cause wills and produces other things inasmuch as it loves the first end, which is nothing but itself. But nothing can be willed which is not known first. Evidently, then, God loves other things because of Himself, namely, inasmuch as He loves Himself. And since He cannot will these things without knowing them, it is necessary that the act by which He knows and loves them be a primary act, like the act by which He knows and loves His own divine essence.

Further, to admit succession and diversity of acts in God is inconceivable and absurd. It would be like introducing accidentality and potentiality into God, and so reduce the absolute perfection of the *primum effectivum,* which demands that God have a most actual knowledge of what He can produce. Not only that, but God has a distinct knowledge of all possible and real beings, prior to any kind of reality they might have or attain. The object of the intellect is being in all its possible extension. Accordingly, only that intellect is perfect which knows, not confusedly, but distinctly and actually, all that in some way or other participates in the nature of being (*ratio entis*). Since the divine intellect is one and the same as the essence of this first cause, it follows that, like the first cause itself, it must be perfectly and necessarily in act. If we now hold that all the beings distinct from the first cause are not necessary—the necessary being is only one—and exist only dependently on the action of the *primum effectivum,* we are bound to admit that the act by which God knows these beings is prior to them: first, because by nature the necessary always precedes the contingent, and second, because the first cause acts only to the extent that it knows.

It is only at this point that Duns Scotus believes that he has at hand the logical elements needed to demonstrate that the first cause is infinite. "Having established these preliminary points, I shall now demonstrate in four ways the infinity [of God]."[116] We shall follow him in this demonstration.

GOD'S INFINITY

The first series of arguments that leads us to attribute infinity to God is based on a truth already acquired, namely, that He is the first cause of all things. If Aristotle's opinion that the world is eternal were true, the infinite power of God would thereby be demonstrated. But while it is difficult to demonstrate with positive arguments that the world has been produced from all eternity, and consequently that its changes are infinite, it is not at all difficult to conceive the possibility on God's part of conserving the world forever. Otherwise stated, it is easy to admit that the first cause can produce an infinity of effects in virtue of its own power and without the help of any other cause.

This question leaves our demonstration intact. In one case as in the other, the first cause must actually possess an infinite power, even though, because of the nature of the effects, it never displays it, or will never be able to display it in its complete possible extension. It is important to keep in mind that

---

[116] *Op. Oxon.,* I, d. 2, q. 2, n. 25.

nothing can happen except by the power of the first cause, in such wise that all efficiency must be brought back to the efficiency of God, whose power is responsible for all real or possible things. If there is no limit in the number of possible effects, there can be no limits in the power that is able to produce them independently of other causes, that is subject to no other power, and that is perfectly actual and without succession.[117]

God, let us repeat, knows even before He acts. Since intelligible beings, just as possible beings, are infinite, it is only logical to say that God knows an infinity of things. Our intellect, too, inasmuch as its object is being in its full extension, enjoys an activity that is somehow unlimited (*quodammodo illimitata*). Yet we cannot say that our intellect is infinite in the way that the divine intellect is infinite. We know one thing after another, in succession; God knows all things simultaneously. He has not only the capacity to know them, but He knows them in act. We arrive at a knowledge of things through a multiplicity of concepts which we can reduce to unity only with difficulty, while the divine intellect knows all things distinctly in the perfect unity of the divine essence. Our intellective act depends not only on the activity of the soul but also on the thing known, whereas the divine intellect knows all things perfectly by virtue of its power alone. Whether things exist or not does not make any difference to the perfection of divine knowledge: the actual existence of things adds nothing to it.

An intellect that knows the whole infinity of possible things in one act, most perfectly, and in virtue of its own power, must be infinite. Just as greater strength is needed to carry ten objects than five, so greater activity is needed to know two things than one. If things are infinite in number, to know them

---

[117] *Ibid*.

all, taken together and yet distinctly, an infinite activity is required.[118]

The two foregoing considerations point to the need of admitting an infinite being at the origin of all things. The two considerations to follow will show that the final cause must also be infinite.

By internal experience we know that our will is never fully satisfied with the goods of this world; it is always ready to seek and love something greater and something better, as soon as an idea of it comes to mind. As is evident, it will rest only in the possession of a good that includes all goods, a good that is all goods together, with no exclusion or succession. Now a good that sums up in itself all goods in a perfect and simultaneous actuality, so that no other good not already contained in it eminently, that is, in the most perfect manner, can exist, is precisely an infinite good. Therefore, it must be said that our will, which has the good for its object, does not flee from an infinite good as from something absurd, but even craves for it with a profound, intimate joy.

The same observation holds true for the intellect. The object of the intellect is being. Our intellect does not shrink from the thought of an infinite being as something contradictory, but, on the contrary, it soon discovers by reflection that only the infinite being is being in the full sense of the term, and that no other being is equally intelligible. No one is more competent to do a certain thing than one born for that particular thing. Hence if the will shows by its way of acting that no other good is equal to the infinite good, and if the intellect shows likewise that no other being is equal to the infinite being, it is clear that the note of infinity conflicts neither with the idea of the good nor with that of being.

Again, when it was established that the first efficient and final cause is first also in the order of perfection, it was proved

[118] *Ibid.,* n. 30.

at the same time that that cause is the most perfect existing
reality. Since the will can always desire a good that is greater
than any finite good, and since the intellect can always think
of a being that is more perfect than any finite being, it is evident that neither good nor being can be truly most perfect
unless it is infinite. Nor can God be truly the supreme final
cause and the first being in the order of perfection unless He
is infinite.[119]

No one will fail to see that these considerations lead to one
conclusion: the infinite must exist because my will desires it
and my intellect conceives it. This statement must of course
be understood within the Augustinian cast of thought that no
adequate explanation can be given for the tendency of the will
and the intellect toward the infinite, unless the infinite actually exists: an affirmation that has no meaning in the Aristotelian gnoseology, for which the idea of the infinite has a
purely negative value.

Thus we realize again that Duns Scotus' gnoseology, characterized by the doctrine of the proper object of the intellect
and the related theory of the univocity of being, makes it possible for him to accept what was most profound and essential
in the Augustinian tradition and to revitalize it in a new
synthesis.

For Duns Scotus the demonstration of God's existence really
ends only at this point. The reason is clear. The first and most
fundamental distinction of being is that determined by the
intrinsic modes of finite and infinite. As has been shown, it is
an absolute distinction with no restriction whatsoever, so that
on the metaphysical plane the infinite being has nothing in
common with the finite being. The transcendence of the former in regard to the latter is complete and perfect. Infinity is
thus for Duns Scotus the radical attribute of God, which,

---

[119] *Ibid.*, n. 31.

more than any other attribute, characterizes Him in his absolute unicity and perfection.[120]

If we keep these observations in mind, we shall readily understand why for the Subtle Doctor the demonstration of God's existence is equivalent to the demonstration of the existence of an infinite being. The result of this procedure is that the first part of theodicy, the demonstration of God's existence, is intimately connected and fused with the second part, that is, the deduction of the absolute attributes of God.

GOD AND THE UNIVERSE

The demonstrative process, by which we ascend from creatures to God, is followed by the opposite process that shows how things proceed from God. For the sake of brevity we shall pass over the doctrines that Duns Scotus holds in common with the whole scholastic tradition, and mention only those characteristic of his system which represent his personal contribution, a new note in the harmonious whole of Christian philosophy.

In showing how created beings proceed from God, Duns Scotus' main preoccupation is to emphasize both God's freedom and the radical contingency of things. God, the most perfect cause of the universe, *habet rationem secundum quam format*,[121] that is, He knows things before He creates them. Hence, from all eternity, He has within Himself the idea of all things He will draw out of nothing or has the power to draw out of nothing. Before conferring existence on things, He has a perfect knowledge of their essence.

These are common notions on which we need not insist further. But what is the foundation of the essence or idea of real and possible things? St. Thomas, as well as the whole

---

[120] *Op. Oxon.*, I, d. 3, q. 2, n. 17.
[121] *Ibid.*, d. 35, q. unica, n. 12.

scholastic tradition before Duns Scotus, explains the origin of the *rationes aeternae* in God in the following way. The divine essence is by nature imitable in infinite ways; hence the intellect that knows perfectly the divine essence, knows it not only in itself but also in its infinite relations of imitability *ad extra*. Thus in the unique and most perfect act by which God knows Himself are contained the idea of God and the ideas of all possible essences, which are but imitations of the divine essence.

Duns Scotus is not completely satisfied with this way of considering the logical moments in the divine knowledge. What he does not like in this theory is the logical priority that possible essences obtain, so to speak, over the act of the divine intellect. If, indeed, the relations of imitability between the divine essence and the essences of created or producible things have their foundation in the divine essence as such, it will no longer be possible to say that God's intellect produces the ideas of things. Rather we shall have to say that the divine intellect simply takes notice of these ideas, which it already finds in itself. On the other hand, it is impossible to know a relationship, which of its nature implies reference to another, without also knowing, in addition to its principle, its terminus. Hence it follows that the divine intellect would somehow be dependent upon things, since they are the termini of the relations that radiate, to use a concrete expression, in all directions from the divine essence.

"This seems to vilify the divine intellect, which in this case becomes passive in regard to the objects known through these *rationes*. The knowledge of these *rationes* on the part of the divine intellect would be determined by the presence of the objects."[122]

Briefly, the reasonableness of things would not only have its foundation in the divine essence, but would in a certain sense

---

[122] *Ibid.*, n. 5.

already be expressed in it. The divine intellect would only have to become conscious of it.

For the divine intellect to enjoy that absolute independence and priority *(primitas)* which belongs to God's activity, it is necessary to place in it the immediate foundation of all ideas. Furthermore, the divine essence is in itself sufficient to beatify God's intellect. This truth, about which no doubt is possible, could not be saved if "the divine essence as such, prescinding from any real or logical relation,"[123] were not the object of the divine intellection which is perfectly one with it.

To avoid such difficulties, one must look at the logical moments of the divine knowledge in a different way. It should be done as follows. In the first moment, God knows His essence as such, namely, as an infinite sea of perfections. In the second moment, He knows producible things, which thus begin to exist inasmuch as they are the objects of God's thought. In the third moment, it may be said that the divine intellect compares the things known with all other intelligibles and with its own intellection. Finally, in the fourth moment it reflects, as it were, upon this relation between the things known and its own intellect.[124] Thus, according to Duns Scotus, God does not know the possibles because they are necessary imitations of the divine essence, but the possibles are imitations of the divine essence because God knows them and produces them *in esse intelligibili*. Accordingly, God creates not merely the existence of things but also their essence. The cause of the former is the act of the divine will; the cause of the latter is the act of the divine intellect.

Evidently, purely possible beings, in the same way as beings actually created, have been known to God from all eternity. Yet we are not thereby authorized to make fanciful suppositions about a so-called *esse essentiae,* or an ideal, eternal exist-

---

[123] *Ibid.*
[124] *Ibid.*, n. 10.

ence of things somehow distinct from the intellect of God. Before their creation, things have no existence except insofar as they are conceived by God. Their eternal reality is to be placed entirely in the reality of the eternal, most actual, divine intellect, to which they are present solely in virtue of its infinite perfection.[125] God knows the essence of things on exactly the same basis as He knows their existence, namely, as an exigency of His most perfect intellect to which nothing can be new or unknown.

In this order of ideas, it will be readily understood that the necessity of the possibles and the essences is not a perfection of things in themselves, but rests exclusively on the perfection of the divine mind. The dependence of things on God is thus total and absolute.

From among the infinity of possible things, the divine will chooses from all eternity the beings that at a certain moment will be called into existence. That all beings, outside of God, are contingent, is a fact of experience as well as a truth of immediate evidence. Whereas on the basis of the previous considerations the existence of finite and contingent beings compels us to affirm the existence of an infinite and necessary being, it is not possible to infer the existence of contingent beings from the existence of God. "Indeed, from the existence of the more perfect it does not follow that the imperfect must also exist."[126] Yet, the proposition that some being is contingent (*aliquod ens esse contingens*) is in itself so evident and certain, that those who deny it "are to be exposed to physical torture until they admit the possibility that they be spared such a torture. They should be treated the same way as those who deny the first principles deserve to be treated."[127]

---

[125] See the whole dist. 36, q. unica, for a thorough discussion of this point.
[126] *Op. Oxon.*, I, d. 39, q. unica, n. 13.
[127] *Ibid.*

We have therefore the right to ask ourselves, without further ado, how is it possible that contingent beings are such, or what is the reason for contingent beings? All Catholic thinkers, observes Duns Scotus, are of the opinion that there could be no contingent being if the first cause had not created at least something *contingenter,* that is, freely. To make contingency in beings depend on the freedom of secondary causes, as Aristotle and Avicenna do, is impossible. In fact, a moving cause that moves inasmuch as it is moved—and this is the case of all causes except the first one—moves necessarily if it is moved necessarily *(si necessario movetur, necessario movet).*[128] Thus if God had produced necessarily the secondary causes, none of them would be able to produce anything freely. But since God acts inasmuch as He knows and wills, the contingency of things will have its root either in His intellect or in His will. The intellect is out of the question, for whatever God knows, He knows necessarily. It remains to be seen what kind of relationship will exist between the divine will and created things, so that these may be called, as they really are, contingent beings.

To speak of will is tantamount to speaking of freedom. A will that is not free is an instinct, an inclination, not a will in the exact meaning of the term. The freedom of the divine will, Duns Scotus points out, does not imply necessarily the possibility of changing its own decisions, which is a sign of imperfection; nor does it imply the possibility of willing and not willing a thing at one and the same time, which is absurd, as it destroys the will; it implies merely that God can will different things in His unique and infinite act. Here an explanation is in order.

The human will is free, for it is not determined to one thing rather than to another and can will two things in succession by two different acts. This succession of acts cannot

_____

[128] *Ibid.,* n. 12.

of course be admitted in the divine will: it is free, but at the same time it is perfectly actual, and therefore immutable. To save these two necessary prerogatives of the divine will, one must say that God embraces by a single act all things that can be willed, even those that are opposed among themselves and can be willed by man only by two distinct acts. If the divine will were inclined only toward certain possible things, it would not be infinite but limited in its act of willing. On the other hand, it cannot be denied that many possible things exclude one another. For example, it is possible for me to be writing at this moment, just as it is possible for me not to be writing; yet, my act of writing excludes its opposite. By one act of the will I can determine myself to write, and by another act I can decide not to write, but I cannot be simultaneously in act in regard to both things together. The human will is thus inde-termined in regard to two things only before it is in act, before it wills. Once I determine myself to one thing, I can no longer be in act in regard to the other. My will is completely possessed, as it were, by the object actually willed.

With regard to God's will, things are different. By exclud-ing from it, as we must, any succession of acts, and by admit-ting that its object is everything that somehow or other can be willed, one must say that God's will, considered both as a power and as an act, does not tend of necessity toward any particular thing, and it is therefore always possible for it to will the opposite of the thing willed. The reason is evident. No other object, apart from the divine essence, can so bind and tie the will of God to itself as to absolutely exclude the willing of its opposite.[129]

---

[129] "I affirm that the divine will does not tend by necessity to any object that is not its own essence. It acts contingently in regard to any other object, so that it could will its opposite. This is true not only when the will is considered in itself before it tends toward that object, or simply as a will, which is naturally anterior to its act, but also when it is considered in the act itself of willing." *Ibid.,* n. 22.

Bearing this in mind, we can now understand the radical contingency of things. In the act of creation God assigned to each thing its own nature: to fire, the power of heating; to water, the property of being cold; to air, the property of being lighter than the earth; and so forth. But precisely because the divine will cannot be bound to any particular object, it is not absurd to conceive the possibility on the part of fire to be cold, of water to be warm, of earth to be lighter than air, and of the entire universe not to exist or to be ruled by entirely different laws. Likewise, when God created the human soul, He gave it such a nature that it can survive the body. Yet it would be equally reasonable and right for the soul to perish together with the body. For all that creatures have and is due to them in virtue of their nature God owes to them not in justice *(ex iustitia)*, but only out of liberality *(ex liberalitate)*.[130]

---

[130] *Op. Oxon.,* IV, d. 46, q. 1, n. 12.

VII

MORAL DOCTRINES

THERE ARE FEW DOCTRINES of Duns Scotus that have not been misunderstood or misinterpreted even by well-meaning scholars. Perhaps the most badly treated of all is his teaching on the relationship between the divine will and created things. The brief reference to this teaching which we have made in the last pages of the preceding chapter must be developed and set in relation to his moral system.

Duns Scotus has been charged with exaggerating God's freedom in regard to creatures to such an extent that, to follow his principles, one might well conclude that the laws of the universe and of morality have no foundation except an absolutely arbitrary divine will. It is true that certain Scotistic texts[131] can be cited in confirmation of this interpretation. But it is also true that a correct and sound exegesis of the thought of a systematic thinker like Duns Scotus cannot be based on the authority of brief and scattered statements taken out of their context. A sound exegesis must try to discover the meaning of a doctrine in the system as a whole. We intend to do this in the present chapter within the usual limits of this study.

---

[131] See for example *Reportata Parisiensia,* IV, d. 46, q. 4, n. 8.

THE DIVINE WILL VS. CREATION AND THE MORAL ORDER

Duns Scotus maintains that the statement, "God wills in a most reasonable and orderly manner" *(Deus est rationabilissime et ordinatissime volens),* is a fundamental and incontestable principle of philosophy.[132] For him this means that it is absolutely impossible to conceive God's free will as something purely arbitrary and capricious. As we shall see presently, God finds in Himself the norm of His willing and acting. The principle, *Operari sequitur esse,* retains for Duns Scotus its value in the sphere of all reality, including the divine reality. Hence neither the act of understanding nor the act of willing can be the radical constituent of the divine nature. In God, as in any other being, *esse* precedes *operari.* On the other hand, the acts of understanding and willing presuppose an object. Thus even from this point of view the divine essence, which is the object of God's intellect and will, must logically precede the acts of these two powers. Since the divine essence is the proper and necessary object of God's will, it must also be its supreme norm. God cannot will anything that is in contrast with His essence; nay, He cannot will anything that does not find its foundation and justification in His essence.[133]

The divine will not only presupposes God's essence, but also the act of His intellect. No doubt, Duns Scotus is always careful to keep the volitional act independent of the intellective act. The act of the will, in God even more than in man, is never determined by the motives presented by the intellect. The voli-

---

[132] A great many passages could be quoted in confirmation. I limit myself to the two following references: *Op. Oxon.,* III, d. 32, q. unica, n. 6; *Rep. Par.,* III, d. 7, q. 4, n. 4.

[133] "Indeed, the divine essence, which is the primary object of that will, is to be willed in itself. Hence that will necessarily and correctly wills that object which is properly to be willed in itself." *Op. Oxon.,* I, d. 10, quaest. unica, n. 11.

tional act receives all its ontological reality from the will to which it belongs by nature. This, however, is not the same as to say that the will can act without any previous knowledge. If it is wrong to attribute the main causality of the volitional act to the intellect, simply because something is willed only after it is known, it is equally wrong to affirm that the will can be truly a will, and not just a blind instinct, without the light of the intellect. By excluding a causal connection between the volitional act and the act of the intellect, the natural connection that holds between the two faculties is not thereby excluded. "Following the natural order existing among the operations of intellect and will, action should follow knowledge."[134] Furthermore, the greater perfection of the divine will in contrast to the human will consists precisely in this, that the divine will can act only in conformity with the dictates of God's most perfect intellect.[135]

The importance of these assertions should not escape the attention of the reader. If knowledge naturally precedes the will, it follows that all analytical judgments and the conclusions that can be derived from them are true antecedently to any act of the will, or at least they are true even if by an absurd hypothesis all acts of the will are excluded, for "knowledge depends essentially only on the power and its object."[136] This holds true not only for the theoretical axioms and principles, but also for the principles of ethics.[137]

---

[134] *Op. Oxon.*, Prologus, q. 4, n. 14.

[135] *Ibid.*, n. 35: "It is a sign of the will's perfection to act always in conformity with the power that precedes it in acting, whenever this power acts first and perfectly in regard to its object."

[136] *Op. Oxon.*, III, d. 24, q. unica, n. 4.

[137] *Op. Oxon.*, Prologus, q. 4, n. 13: "The truth of a practical and necessary principle does not in effect depend on the will more than does the truth of a speculative principle. The same must be said of the conclusions that are drawn necessarily from such a principle."

Since the perfection of the divine will demands that whatever it wills be in conformity with truth, it is evident that in His willing and acting God is bound, as it were, by the truth. Hence God will not be able to will the absurd, nor will He be able not to will that which is necessary.

Thus Duns Scotus is perfectly consistent with his own teaching when he affirms that only "that which does not include a contradiction is *per se* nonrepugnant to the divine will,"[138] and that "the infinite will wills necessarily an infinite object,"[139] and "loves necessarily its own goodness."[140] Also, along with its own essence, the divine will must love with a love of complacency all possible things that the intellect presents to it, inasmuch as each one of them is somehow a participation of its own goodness (*quaedam participatio bonitatis propriae*).[141]

This statement helps us make a step forward in the inquiry as to how things proceed from God. The love of complacency by which God loves all the possibles makes it evident that God must approve as good all producible essences. When He actually creates them, He must make them in accordance with their mode of being. This means that these essences will have all the essential perfections that belong to them and all those relations of the metaphysical, physical, and moral order that bind them together. However, reality is not merely the sum-total of essential perfections, necessary properties, and inevitable relations. Upon this canvas of perfections and necessary relations we can observe the intertwining of a wonderful variety of colors and shades, with an infinite richness of particulars, all contingent and accidental, from which the magnificent and complex system of the universe is derived. Is it here then that

[138] *Rep. Par.,* IV, d. 46, q. 4, n. 8.
[139] *Quodlib.,* q. 16, n. 9.
[140] *Ibid.,* n. 7.
[141] *Ibid.*

the divine will chooses, orders, and determines capriciously and without consulting beforehand His divine wisdom?

It is impossible to think, protests Duns Scotus, that God acts this way. He is an infinitely wise architect who knows His own work in all its particulars, piece by piece, in itself, and in its relation to the whole.[142] Accordingly, even those things and events which appear to us as negligible and meaningless enter into God's absolutely perfect design and are parts of it. They are like individual notes in the immense harmony of the universe.

Perhaps no medieval thinker felt as deeply as did Duns Scotus the need and exigency for order and design in God's mind and His works. One might say that his conviction, which is part of his other conviction previously mentioned, namely, that God is *rationabilissime et ordinatissime volens,* is the directive idea, the light that guides Duns Scotus in his meditation on the mysteries of God and creation. The fecundity of such an idea is clearly indicated by the sublimity of his theological intuitions.[143] To sum up, we must say that the existence or nonexistence of a contingent thing depends entirely on the free will of God, but once God wills and creates, He must necessarily will and create wisely and orderly.

It goes without saying that it would be foolish for us to pretend to know, always and completely, the reasons of God's infinite wisdom. It is enough for us to know that, although God established an order in creation, He is not necessarily bound by it. His divine will loves necessarily only one thing, His own supreme goodness. Hence, whatever God may will, even if it is above the actually existing order, both on the natural and on the supernatural plane, it will always be within

[142] *Rep. Par.,* I, d. 36, q. 4, nn. 11 and 22.

[143] Cf. Ephrem Longpré, *La Philosophie du B. Duns Scot* (Paris: Société et Librairie S. François d'Assise, 1924), p. 62, n. 4.

the supreme laws of that necessary order according to which His will is related to His essence.

Thus Scotistic voluntarism in reference to God is found to consist exclusively in the fact that it draws the natural consequences of what is taught by all Catholic thinkers, namely, that the works *ad extra* are only the secondary object of the divine will. If it is true that God loves necessarily only Himself, and if, on the other hand, it is true that no created thing can force itself upon God by virtue of an intrinsic necessity—for, in this case, He would need it for His own perfection and happiness—it must also be true that God not only can will without contradiction a world different from the present one, but He can also modify the present order and dispose things in such a way that they would tend toward Him otherwise than they actually do. What He cannot will is that creatures will not be ordained to Him.

THE DETERMINANTS OF MORALITY

The most serious objection leveled against so-called Scotistic voluntarism is that it leads to a moral positivism that may be expressed something like this: right and wrong depend exclusively on the will of God; what God wills is right, what God forbids is wrong. The best and most effective answer to this objection can be found in some of the basic principles of Scotistic ethics.

We can consider things in two different ways: in their own reality, that is, in themselves, or in their relation to other things. When considered in themselves, things are always good. The more perfect is their being, the better they are. This is what is called their metaphysical goodness. It is that kind of goodness which, according to the philosophical axiom, is convertible with being (*ens et bonum convertuntur*). When a thing is looked at from the viewpoint of the relations it has here and now to other things, it is said to be good or bad only relatively. Its goodness or lack of goodness depends on whether its presence and action in given circumstances is or is not in harmony with the exigencies of its own nature, whether it does or does not respect the necessary relations it has to other things. Duns Scotus calls this secondary goodness to distinguish it from metaphysical goodness. He defines it thus: "The secondary goodness of being, which is accidental and accruing to being, is its integral harmony with other things to which it is necessarily related, or the harmony of other things to itself."[144] Moral goodness belongs to this type of goodness.

The moral goodness of an act, remarks Duns Scotus, is not something that belongs to the act considered in its metaphysical entity, but rather to the act considered in relation to all those things that constitute the sum-total of its circumstances.[145] Moral goodness can therefore be called the proportion that the act has to its power and object, as well as its end, time, place, and mode,[146] which are the concomitant circumstances of every act. Let us examine the role that each of these elements—*potentia, objectum, finis, tempus, locus, et modus*—plays in the constitution of the moral act.

As to the part that a power plays in the constitution of the moral act, Duns Scotus has nothing new to say. The necessary requirement for an act to be moral is that it be free. It must proceed from a rational power, having not only the consciousness of its own act, but also control over it. Following his own psychology, Duns Scotus takes care to emphasize in this connection, that while the consciousness of the act belongs to the intellect, dominion over the act, and hence its responsibility (*imputabilitas*), belongs to the will. For the will alone pos-

---

[144] *Quodlib.*, q. 18, n. 3.
[145] *Op. Oxon.*, I, d. 17, q. 3, n. 2.
[146] *Rep. Par.*, II, d. 40, q. unica, n. 3.

sesses that indifference or indeterminacy with regard to contra-
dictories in which freedom properly consists.[147]

The role assigned by Duns Scotus to the object deserves
more detailed consideration. It is when the act is looked at
from the aspect of its relation to the object that it begins to
acquire a meaning and value in the field of morality. If freedom makes the act capable of acquiring a moral value, what
confers the actuality of being good or evil on it and thus brings
it *de facto* into the field of morality, is primarily the object.
"The primary [moral goodness] belongs to the volitive act
insofar as it directs itself toward an object which is proper to it,
not only according to the natural order of things, but also
according to the dictates of right reason."[148] This is such an
important statement that a short commentary on it will not be
out of place.

In order that an act, toward which a man is consciously and
freely determined, may be called good, it is required, first, that
the act have as its terminus an object which in itself is a value,
or a real good for the agent; and secondly, that this relation
of agreement and perfectibility between the acting power and
the moving object be known and willed. When either one of
these two conditions is missing, the act can no longer be called
good.

An important consequence follows from this. A man may
erroneously, but with a sure conscience, judge that a morally
valuable object is without moral value, and yet act with the
intention of obtaining it. His act, according to Scotus, cannot
be called good. The reason is that, in spite of his opposite
conviction, the object "is not by its nature in agreement with
the will." In other words, for Duns Scotus it is not enough that
the judgment of conscience be sure; it must also be objectively
correct. However, one should not be led to believe that in order

---

[147] *Quodlib.*, q. 18, n. 9.
[148] *Op. Oxon.*, II, d. 7, q. unica, n. 11.

to grasp an object's agreement or lack of agreement with the will an exact quidditative knowledge of the object is required. Such knowledge is usually rare and difficult to obtain. While the agreement of the act with the power that performs it is immediately evident, it is enough that the agreement of the object with the power be known by experience. Briefly, it is not necessary to have scientifically perfect knowledge, but only practical knowledge.

Yet the object alone cannot be the absolute determinant of the morality of an act. Everyone knows, for example, that when I give alms to the poor with the intention of showing my wealth rather than of doing a charitable act, I perform an act of vanity. Duns Scotus bears witness to the dictate of our conscience when he states: "Secondary moral goodness belongs to the volitive act inasmuch as it is performed by the will having due consideration of all the circumstances."[149] That is, before I can determine whether an action is good or evil, I must take into consideration the circumstances of place and time, the way in which it has been or is going to be accomplished, and especially the intention of the will that is behind it. "Goodness, as far as circumstances are concerned," affirms Duns Scotus, "depends primarily on the end."[150]

Evidently, as should be clear from our previous statements, a right intention alone is not sufficient to make an act good. Yet it must be admitted that no action is good in the full sense of the term, unless it be ordained to an end that is worth being pursued by man, the moral agent. Hence a further problem arises: what is the end that is truly worth being pursued, and toward which man must direct his actions? It is clear that not any end whatsoever can confer moral dignity on man's actions, but only an end that represents man's supreme value.

[149] *Ibid.*
[150] *Ibid.*, d. 40, q. unica, n. 3.

Duns Scotus does not hesitate for a moment to affirm that God alone is the true and ultimate end of all man's activity. Only the man who ordains all his actions to God respects and realizes in himself the proper hierarchy of values that lead to God. Man's will finds its basis and model in the divine will. God's sanctity demands that He love the supreme goodness of His own essence and other things only insofar as they participate in it and are ordained to it. In the same way, there can be no true sanctity in man if he loves anything that is not ordained to God.[151] Therefore, to act merely for the sake of virtue, as if virtue were good in itself, would amount to placing virtue on a par with God as an absolute value close to another absolute value, an end close to another end. Man would thus break the natural hierarchy of values, all of which are ordained to God.

A more definite condemnation of so-called autonomous morality can hardly be found. For Duns Scotus, just as for St. Augustine, virtue is not something valuable simply because it is a way of acting that is measured by, and in accordance with, nature, as Aristotle teaches, but because of the act of love by which the virtuous act is directed to God.

Thus far the Subtle Doctor does not go beyond traditional ethics. Yet even in expounding the principles and doctrines common to Christian tradition, he does not fail to leave the marks of his systematic and scientific mind. He is not satisfied with studying one by one the constitutive elements of morality, but he presents them within the framework of a well-determined structure. In the moral act, object and circumstances, among which the end is the chief, are related to one another by a relation analogous to that existing between matter and form in real being, and between genus and specific

---

[151] *Ibid.*, I, d. 48, q. unica, n. 2: "Every act of our will [action, thought] is above all ordained to the final end, which is the Alpha and Omega, the beginning and the end, to Whom be honor and glory *in saecula saeculorum. Amen.*"

difference in logical being. The object that is "in accord with the dictates of right reason" confers on the act only a generic goodness, which, to be complete, needs that further determination which comes to it mainly from the end.[152] Hence morality results from the goodness of the object and the goodness of the end. If either one of these two is missing, an act cannot be called a morally good act.

MORALLY INDIFFERENT ACTS

It cannot be denied that Scotus' foregoing statements represent a remarkable effort of penetrative insight into what may be called the metaphysical structure of morality. They have to be kept in mind by him who wishes to grasp the meaning of certain ethical opinions that are specifically Scotistic in character. Thus the Subtle Doctor distinguishes between what he calls contrary malice and privative malice. It is necessary to explain what he means by this.

If my will directs itself toward an object which is not in accord with human dignity, I perform an act that is evil *contrarie*. In so doing, I not only do not positively tend toward my end, but I turn toward something that is opposed to it. To be more specific, I do exactly the opposite of what I ought to do. On the contrary, if the object of my action is good, but I tend to it without ordering it at least indirectly to the final end, my action will be privatively evil, for it will lack the goodness that is due to it. In this case, my act will be a good act only generically, since it falls short of the goodness of the end which is a sort of specific difference for it. Apart from the specific difference, no being is really what it is; so also no act is really good unless it be ordained to its proper end. Acts that are privatively evil may also be called indifferent acts.[153]

---

[152] *Op. Oxon.*, II, d. 7, q. unica, n. 11.
[153] *Ibid.*, n. 13.

The reason is this. An act that is privatively evil *(malus privative)* is neither contrary to the end nor positively ordained to it; it causes us to make neither a step forward nor a step backward. Thus, generally speaking, an act must be called morally indifferent when it is accomplished without a moral end, or, which is even more important from the practical point of view, when the end or motive inspiring it does not attain the moral standard that is due to a good act, even though it is not evil in itself.

A created object can always be willed for a morally insufficient end. Only God, the infinite good, confers perfect moral value on the act that has a relation to Himself, for in God object and end are identical, and he who loves God tends necessarily towards his due end. In other words, by its nature a created object can confer only generic morality on an act. On the other hand, love of God is always a morally perfect act, for in it the object is identical with that primary end which constitutes goodness itself.

Is it possible to have morally indifferent acts in the concrete? As is well known, Duns Scotus and St. Thomas are not of one opinion on this point. While St. Thomas answers the question in the negative, Duns Scotus favors a positive answer.[154] The roots of the disagreement are to be found in their different ways of evaluating the importance of the judgment of our conscience. For St. Thomas, an action performed with a sure, even though erroneous, conscience, is either good or evil; for Duns Scotus, an act is really good only when the goodness of the object and the goodness of the end agree. If for any reason, such as ignorance or lack of due consideration, an act is not positively ordained to the end, it fails to reach that standard of goodness which holds for every act, not only generically, but also specifically.

---

[154] *Ibid.,* d. 41, q. unica, n. 4.

A clue to the solution of the problem can perhaps be found in the observation that neither St. Thomas nor Duns Scotus adverted to the fact that not every human act, even though conscious and free, is *ipso facto* a moral act. If I think only of the esthetic and economic values of an act and pay no heed whatsoever, not even confusedly, to its moral value, my act will be a human act, but not a moral one. Hence one will easily concede to St. Thomas that in order to be good an act does not need to be performed expressly out of a virtuous motive or the love of God. It will be enough to advert to its ethical goodness in general. On the other hand, it will not be difficult to accept Duns Scotus' viewpoint that not all human acts, simply because they are the result of a conscious and free decision, are to be called good or evil. However, neither may they be called *morally* indifferent acts. They are simply acts that do not attain to the level of ethical values.

Our conscience tells us clearly that if good is always to be done, still not all good is to be done. In other words, our conscience is witness to the fact that the sphere of the good and the sphere of duty do not always and necessarily coincide. To understand the saying, *Bonum est faciendum,* in the sense that an action, because of the very fact that it is good, is also obligatory, would lead us to an impossible rigorism. As can be proved from many passages in his works, Duns Scotus was well aware of this phenomenological datum of conscience. It is certainly good for man to direct all his actions to God; better, it is precisely in this that the essence of good lies, as we have seen before. Nevertheless, Scotus writes: "Man is not bound always to refer his acts to God by an actual or virtual intention, for God did not oblige us to do so."[155] The reason why God did not oblige man to do all possible good deeds is that "God did not wish to oblige man to do the impossible,

---

[155] *Ibid.*

or what is too difficult for him in his earthly condition."[156]
The testimony of our conscience that duty and the good do not
coincide finds its confirmation in the traditional distinction
between precepts and evangelical counsels. The former are
obligatory for everybody; the latter are free. Here arise certain
problems concerning the nature and extent of duty, which will
be discussed in the next section.

DUTY AND THE NATURAL LAW

When is good to be done? When do good and duty coincide? On what basis does the good become obligatory? A first
observation to be made is that the moral obligation to perform an act can be founded either on the necessary relation
of the object to the agent, or on its imposition by a superior
will. Does the obligation of the moral act have its foundation in the necessary relation of the object or merely in the
command of God?

Duns Scotus' thought on this point is clear and definite. The
divine essence, which is a necessary good for God's will, is
also a necessary good for every rational creature. God is the
last end toward which all creatures are ordained, either directly
or indirectly, in virtue of their very nature as creatures. God
alone is a necessary good, lovable in Himself. Being the source
of goodness, He is also the source of duty. Other goods outside
of God become obligatory only to the extent that they help
man attain his end and thus participate in the obligation binding man to God. Hence a sin is committed not only when a
man departs from his end, but also when he disregards means
necessary to the attainment of that end. Contempt of the
means jeopardizes the end, just as the intellect's rejection of
a conclusion implies negation of the principle from which the
conclusion is derived.[157]

---

[156] *Ibid.*, IV, d. 4, q. 4, n. 4.
[157] *Ibid.*, II, d. 37, q. 1, n. 8.

These few remarks may suffice to help us understand that for Duns Scotus duty can only be motivated by the objectively necessary good, God, inasmuch as He is the ultimate and necessary end of all things. They may also help us understand that for the Subtle Doctor a good is obligatory only to the extent that it is an indispensable means to the attainment of the end.

How will man know which goods are obligatory and which are not? How does duty become manifest to my conscience? Duty manifests itself through law. Law and duty are correlative terms. To establish the range of one is to set limits to the other. Duns Scotus has been charged with denying the natural law, or that law which is but the expression of an eternal divine ordination. This charge is undeserved. In fact, differences between Scotistic and traditional doctrine are due to the more rigorous and precise concept of natural law elaborated by the Subtle Doctor. For a law to be called natural in the strict sense of the term, remarks Duns Scotus, it is necessary that it be imposed upon all men, regardless of time, place, customs, and mentality, and with absolute clarity, immediacy, and certainty. These requirements can be met only by practical judgments that are absolutely evident. Accordingly, the natural law, in the strict sense of the term, can only include those ethical axioms which are evident by the simple enunciation of their terms, and those conclusions which can be derived by logical necessity from them.[158] These characteristics are proper only to the first three commandments of the decalogue. Not even God can dispense men from them, for God can will everything except what is absurd or self-contradictory. "These [commandments] belong to the natural law in the strict sense, for, if God exists, it *necessarily* follows that He must be

---

[158] *Op. Oxon.,* III, d. 37, q. unica, n. 1: "Those things are of the natural law which are either necessary principles evident from their terms, or conclusions that follow necessarily from such principles."

loved as God, and no other thing can be the object of divine worship."[159]

In Duns Scotus' opinion, the commandments given on the second stone table also belong to the natural law, but only when it is taken in a broad sense. None of these commandments is immediately evident as an axiom, nor can it be said that they are able to be deduced by logical necessity from the commandments relating to God, or from other ethical axioms. How, then, does Duns Scotus proceed so as to fit these precepts into the natural law and attribute to them a universal value equal to that of the commandments of the first table?[160]

On this point Duns Scotus' thought is not quite clear and accurate. He gives two reasons. The first is the particular harmony that exists between the commandments of the second table and those of the first. This harmony is much deeper than the one existing between positive law and ethical axioms. The second reason is derived from the traditional teaching that all the commandments have been impressed by God on the human heart. From a philosophical point of view, it is evident that the first reason is much more appealing than the second, which has a rather theological flavor.

A more effective way of establishing the foundation of this universal acknowledgment of the natural law taken in a broad sense might consist in the ease with which a man admits the need for such commandments, once he considers the tragic consequences that would ensue upon their nonobservance.[161]

---

[159] *Ibid.*, n. 6.

[160] *Ibid.*, n. 14; *Rep. Par.*, II, d. 22, q. unica, n. 3.

[161] This is the acute observation made by P. F. Schwendinger in his fundamental study of Scotus' ethics, "Metaphysik des Sittlichen nach J. Duns Scotus," *Wissenschaft und Weisheit*, I (1934), 180-210; II (1935), 18-50; III (1936), 93-119; 161-190, which I use here as a basis for my exposition.

Duns Scotus makes use of this criterion in establishing the basis of man's natural right to private property. In the state of innocence there was no need for private property, for peaceful coexistence based on the common moderation of desires was enough to insure basic material goods to everyone. After original sin, establishment of the right to private property became necessary because of man's greed, violence, and sloth.[162]

The reasons justifying the Scotistic distinction between the natural law in the strict sense and the natural law in a broader sense can be reduced to three.

1. A keen mind like Duns Scotus' could not fail to notice the different force with which the commandments of the first table and those of the second table are imposed.

2. Sacred Scripture presents us with cases in which God, in view of a superior good, dispenses from one or the other commandment of the second table. But not even the absolute power of God can shake the objective metaphysical necessity that underlies all ethical axioms and the conclusions strictly derived from them. Hence we must conclude that if God dispenses from a precept, the implication is that such a precept does not rest upon a metaphysical necessity, nor can it find its adequate expression in a necessary judgment. A truly natural law cannot be tampered with, not even by the will of God.

3. However, the fundamental reason for the distinction between the two kinds of precepts of the natural law lies in Duns Scotus' metaphysics of value. Only the infinite being is good in itself; all other beings are good only to the extent that they are ordained to God. Now it is clear that the ethics of duty is but a reflex, a consequence, of the metaphysics of the good. A thing must be good in order to be of obligation, and the better a thing is, the greater is its obligation. If God

---

[162] *Op. Oxon.*, IV, d. 15, q. 2, n. 4.

then is the good in itself, the very essence of goodness, only God must be loved in an absolute manner and only God can be the object of necessary duties. Created things do not possess perfect goodness, for they are morally good only to the extent that they are ordained to the last end. Hence they cannot impose any obligation, except insofar as they are necessary means to the last end. Which creature, Duns Scotus asks pertinently, can attribute to itself "a goodness that is necessary for the goodness of the last end?"[163] Which creature can claim to be necessary for the realization of the goals of God's infinite wisdom? Thus, in the last analysis, it is the limitation of their value that prevents creatures from being the object of necessary and absolute duties. The commandments of the second table, and all the duties that are in any way related to them, concern precisely the relations of men among themselves, and have as their object certain created goods. In accord with traditional teaching, Duns Scotus makes them part of the natural law. On account of his particular views on the subject, he adopts in their regard the denomination of natural law "in a broad sense."

POSITIVE LAW AND CONFIRMATORY LAW

Besides natural law, Duns Scotus discusses positive law and what he calls confirmatory law. The characteristic traits of positive laws are the object of a very careful study on his part, and are as follows. Positive laws do not belong to the field of natural law, nor are they related to it by a consequential relation or by way of a necessary corollary. They are rather integrations of the natural law, required by its indeterminateness as to the changing conditions and complex situations in which men find themselves in concrete life. However, the natural

---

[163] *Ibid.*, III, d. 37, q. unica, n. 5.

law, as a negative norm, always remains as the basis of all positive laws. Such laws would lose all value if they contained anything contrary to the natural law.

The fact that positive laws are not what might be called evident, or at least easily deduced, conclusions from the natural law explains their character of historical and geographical mutability. Certain positive laws may be valid only for a certain period of time or some particular historical situation. On the other hand, since positive laws do not derive their binding force directly from the natural law, the problem naturally arises as to the basis of their legitimacy and value. To put it in another way, if nature is not the basis of the positive laws, what legislator has within himself the authority to impose such obligations upon men?

Evidently, the title of legislator belongs primarily to God. That He actually exercised such a right is plain from a reading of the Scriptures. The Church also, by God's direct delegation, has the right to promulgate and impose positive laws within the limits of its spiritual and religious power. That legislative power likewise belongs to the state is not difficult to demonstrate. Such a power derives from the authority that at one time the natural law gave to a father of a family. In Scotus' opinion, states are but a development of the large patriarchal families, in which authority resided by right of nature in the head of the family. When later the human race grew and spread and peoples of different blood mingled together, the family system became impossible. Henceforth, the chief of the newly formed social groups was no longer designated by right of patriarchal descent, but was elected and appointed by the free choice of the people. The election system changed, but the authority of the ruler always rested on that natural hierarchical exigency that had established the authority of the head of the family.[164] The act, then, by which the legislator promulgates the law that he has decreed in his prudence is the foundation or source of the law's binding force.

Positive confirmatory law has in common with all positive laws the fact that it is promulgated by a legislator. However, its content is identical with the natural law taken both in its strict and broad sense. Although a human legislator can also promulgate positive laws to confirm certain duties already imposed by the natural law, only God can promulgate a truly confirmatory law having the same characteristic of universality as the law of nature. For this reason, Duns Scotus includes in the category of positive confirmatory laws only such Old Testament legislation as confirms and determines the natural law.

That God alone can be the legislator of positive confirmatory law is manifest from the ties binding this law to the natural law. Because of the identity of the content of the confirmatory law with the norms engraved in our hearts and revealed to us by the voice of our conscience, some may be led to believe that confirmatory law is superfluous. Entirely apart from its contradiction of the solemn promulgation on Mount Sinai, this objection does not constitute a real difficulty for Duns Scotus. He forcefully emphasizes the nonanalytic character, and hence the nonimmediate and necessary evidence, of the ethical judgments, which, taken together, make up the natural law in the broad sense of the term. Bearing this in mind, it will be readily seen that confirmatory law not only is not superfluous, but very convenient and even necessary. Through it, the law of nature can fully shine in the consciences of men and dissipate from their minds the obscurities

---

[164] Cf. P. Parthenius Minges, O.F.M., *Ioannis Duns Scoti Doctrina Philosophica et Theologica* (Quaracchi: Typographia Collegii S. Bonaventurae, 1930), vol. I, pp. 417-21.

and uncertainties likely to arise when they get away from the principles of immediate evidence and rely upon deductions that do not appear to be absolutely necessary.[165] On the other hand, because of its universality, natural law may often appear to be indeterminate. Hence its clarification or authentic interpretation will be very helpful. In relation to natural law, positive confirmatory law is like a positive approval and clarification. This can be done authoritatively only by God, the author of nature.

The utility and efficacy of the confirmatory law will be manifest to anyone who reflects upon the concrete psychology of the human soul. It is beyond doubt that if God's express command is added to the dictate of our conscience, we are more deeply impressed by it. Our sense of duty will also become stronger and clearer. This holds for the natural law in the strict sense, and even more so for the natural law in a broad sense, which does not enjoy the immediate evidence that is proper to the former. If to this we add the fact that some men, because of their passions and the dullness of their mind may not even attain a sufficient knowledge of the natural law, just as they do not attain a proper knowledge of God,[166] we shall have an additional reason for emphasizing the importance and necessity of the confirmatory law.

Man's salvation depends upon the attainment of his ultimate end and his journey to this goal is primarily shown to him by the natural law. Hence no one will fail to see how well it befits the divine goodness to provide man with a way of obtaining a knowledge of the natural law that is as clear and

---

[165] *Rep. Par.,* IV, d. 28, q. unica, n. 15: "I wish to emphasize that [the positive confirmatory law] must be promulgated by God, for those things that are far away from the practical principles do not appear to belong to the natural law. The same must be said of those practical principles that are known to everybody by the statement of their terms, whenever these terms are not understood."

[166] *Op. Oxon.,* III, d. 37, q. unica, n. 13.

as effective as possible. The confirmatory positive law is thus an effect of God's paternal solicitude for man.

CONCLUDING REMARKS

In bringing this chapter to a close, two observations are in order. The first is this. The brief exposition that has been made of Duns Scotus' ethics will show how flimsy and crude is the charge of moral positivism sometimes brought against his ethical system. It is plain that for him the basis of morality and the source of moral duty are the divine essence, inasmuch as it is the supreme good and necessary final end of every act and volition. While the ethical axiom "God is to be loved" (*Deus est diligendus*) is, in all its evidence and necessity, the inner strength of all laws, the divine goodness is the cause and source of all values. A more objective and solid foundation of ethics does not seem to be possible.

Scotistic ethics is an attempt to show by way of rigorous demonstration that goodness and duty do not exist, nor have they any significance, apart from their relation to supreme goodness and duty. It is precisely in this that its character and originality lie. This doctrine is distinct from other traditional doctrines, but in substantial agreement with them.

To say that for Duns Scotus the basis of morality is the will of God, is by no means incorrect. But care should be taken not to confuse this will with caprice or arbitrariness. It should rather be understood as that kind of will whereby God *est rationabilissime et ordinatissime volens*.

The second observation is this. Duns Scotus' ethical doctrines offer to us once more the opportunity of discerning how faithful he is to the Augustinian tradition. Indeed, if we were trying to express in a few words the profound conviction inspiring all the analysis and every conclusion of his ethics, we would have to state it thus: just as the love of God for his creatures is the ultimate reason for creation, so the love of man for God is the inner force that raises him to God. Love is thus the law of our being as well as the law of our salvation. Duns Scotus' ethics can rightly be called a scientific demonstration of the primacy of love.

PART THREE

DUNS SCOTUS IN HISTORY
AND CATHOLIC THOUGHT

I

DUNS SCOTUS' POSITION IN THE PAST

PERHAPS IT IS no exaggeration to call Duns Scotus unfortunate because of adverse circumstances that affected both his life and thought. He died before the final revision of his principal work, and left behind him a confused literary legacy which gave rise to very difficult and almost insoluble problems in the systematic study of his teaching. The high prestige reached by St. Thomas in the history of Christian thought is another factor that has contributed to the Subtle Doctor's misfortune. The comparison which becomes so natural, if not necessary, between the Dominican Master and the Franciscan ends up most of the time to Scotus' discredit. Both were profound and systematic thinkers, but St. Thomas has an easy victory because of the clarity of his style, the simplicity of his exposition, and the convincing tone of his argumentation.

These advantages of form and style are far from being negligible. They have done much to make the works of the Angelic Doctor highly readable and quite adaptable as an official textbook in Catholic schools. This fact in turn has led Catholic scholars to focus their attention on the thought of St. Thomas and make it the object of numberless studies and inquiries from the historical, exegetical, and philosophical points of view. The richness, harmony, and fecundity of St.

Thomas' speculation have thus been acknowledged by everyone. All other medieval thinkers, including the gigantic St. Augustine, more often named than really known, and the seraphic St. Bonaventure, have been left in the shadow. Duns Scotus has suffered even more. Not only has his personality been left in the shadow, but of his philosophical and theological works—never studied with that minimum of sympathy which alone makes possible the understanding of a thinker, and never evaluated in a well-balanced and profound vision of the whole system—only those theses have been consistently emphasized which make him appear a systematic opponent of St. Thomas and seem to jar with that harmonious Thomistic synthesis which is the object of universal admiration and is believed to represent the acme and most mature fruit of Christian thought.

Duns Scotus has been reckoned and dismissed as a stubborn and extravagant critic, rather than as a constructive and systematic thinker and a faithful servant of truth from whom one may dissent only after he has been given the credit of a hearing. Thus a new Duns Scotus has been born, the kind of Duns Scotus we know from the manuals of the history of philosophy, especially those written by Catholics, which give little credit to the Subtle Doctor and dismiss him with the usual appellation of an hypercritical mind.

All the charges leveled against Duns Scotus may be summed up in the historical statement that with him scholasticism goes sharply and swiftly into decline. With him, it is said, criticism prevails over constructive thought; the scholastic method, hitherto simple and orderly, becomes confused, subtle, tortuous, and extremely verbose; dialectics supersedes depth of thought, and desire for novelty takes the place of the search for truth.

Following the strong defense of some Franciscan scholars, who called the attention of impartial medievalists to the true meaning of Scotistic speculation, tributes paid to Duns Scotus' deeply constructive genius are increasing every day. Even in Catholic manuals of the history of philosophy, such as Thonnard's and Copleston's,[1] Scotus' philosophical synthesis is now placed among the great systems, in line with those of St. Thomas and St. Bonaventure.

I feel confident that the pages of this brief outline of Duns Scotus' philosophical thought will in some measure help the reader to catch a glimpse of the passion for constructive thinking that pervades all of Scotus' genuine works, a passion that, by universal acknowledgment, animates his theological speculation and produces its most stupendous fruits in the great theses of the Immaculate Conception of Mary and the absolute primacy of Christ.

Real difficulties concerning equally real problems can always be found at the root of all the divergencies between Duns Scotus and the other great scholastic masters. Subtlety of reasoning is but an attempt to embrace the entire complex of a particular problem so as to get a deeper insight into reality. A thinker like Duns Scotus who elaborates such doctrines as the doctrine of the univocity of being, who gives so ingenious and challenging a solution to the problem of knowledge, who places on a new basis the problem of God's existence by exploiting and fusing together all the elements offered to him by tradition, who throws such penetrating light on the problems of ethics, who leaves his mark of originality in all doctrines, who attempts to reconcile in a new synthesis the twofold philosophical tradition that under different names pervades the whole history of human thought, certainly should not be deemed the harbinger of scholasticism's decline.

---

[1] F. J. Thonnard, A.A., *A Short History of Philosophy,* trans. Edward Maziarz, C.PP.S. (Paris-Tournai: Desclée, 1955), pp. 434-52; Frederick Copleston, S.J., *A History of Philosophy* (Westminster: The Newman Press, 1950), vol. II, pp. 476-551.

The reader who has the courage to persevere in the study of his works, which are truly difficult on account of their abstract style and the textual confusion in which they have reached us, will find in Duns Scotus a tenacious researcher, not easily satisfied, but always full of deference toward others, even when new solutions are suggested that follow a new and somewhat different path. The reader will also gain impressions like those one has on entering an unfinished cathedral. The main architectural lines have been almost completely carried out, but while in one place he meets with a spire rising high into the sky, a few steps further he will notice an architectonic motif which has scarcely been hinted at. Wherever he goes, his eyes fall upon scaffolding, beams, materials, and tools that are ready to be used but meanwhile lie without order on the ground or on the scaffolding. The first impression is unavoidably one of disorder. The result is that, while a hasty or unqualified visitor immediately leaves the place dissatisfied, another, who has the time and will to complete mentally the unfinished design on the traces of what has been done, will be able to admire the harmony of the edifice and the architect's creative power. In my opinion, the widely different judgments passed on Duns Scotus' philosophy find their explanation in this fact: Duns Scotus is a thinker who needs, as it were, to be discovered and helped by our attention and understanding.

With regard to the historical meaning of Duns Scotus' speculation, I believe I have made myself sufficiently clear in Part One, Chapter III, of this work. It is always difficult to determine precisely to what extent an original thinker belongs to this or that philosophical trend of thought. However, I am convinced there is good reason for saying that Duns Scotus, in keeping with the speculative tradition of the Franciscan Order, remains substantially an Augustinian. This refers particularly to his way of understanding and stating the various philosophical problems. As occasion has arisen, I have pointed out how strong and profoundly active is the Augustinian inheritance in Duns Scotus' system. To insist further on this point is to no purpose, since I would expose myself to useless repetition. I wish rather to make one observation of a general character.

Everyone knows that the first step toward the understanding and proper evaluation of a doctrine is to see exactly what problem this doctrine aims to solve. It is equally evident that in order to have a good view of anything, we must place ourselves in a convenient place. To neglect to do this is to expose ourselves to the risk of misjudging the object or at least of not completely grasping its value, even if it happens to be a masterpiece. Many scholars have gained the impression that some of Duns Scotus' original philosophical theses are so different and revolutionary in character that they can hardly be understood. This is because they fail to look at them from the proper viewpoint, which is that of the speculative Augustinian tradition. The doctrines of the univocity of being, the formal distinction, knowledge of the singular, and voluntarism, even though expressed in Aristotelian terms and formulas, find their justification and acquire meaning only if linked to problems stated by, and framed within, the Augustinian speculation. To understand Duns Scotus, one must arrive at him by way of Alexander of Hales and St. Bonaventure. This holds for the Subtle Doctor's philosophy as well as for his theology.

As a matter of fact, the discrepancies between two trends of thought, even prior to the solution of a problem, have their roots in the very statement of the problem at issue. To criticize the solution without paying attention to the terms in which the problem is stated is to expose oneself to the risk of committing serious injustice to the thinker under study. Injustice of this kind has been committed by many of Duns Scotus' critics.

When I say that Duns Scotus is substantially an Augustinian, I mean that Scotistic philosophy is nothing but an attempt to offer more precise, more critical, and more scientific solutions to problems perceived in an Augustinian way and within the Augustinian tradition. This need for precision and this scientific spirit can perhaps find their explanation in the natural endowment of Duns Scotus' genius. Yet we should not lose sight of the fact that they were already, so to speak, in the air, impregnated as it was with the name and doctrines of Aristotle. In fact, Aristotle's greatness and the fascination of his works lie mainly in the clarity of his exposition and in the precision of his statements, namely, in that scientific method which he formulated in his logical works and applied in his philosophical treatises.

Furthermore, St. Thomas' example could not but exert influence upon later thinkers. This may explain why Duns Scotus also turned to Aristotle, the master of clarity and precision, in an effort to systematize his own philosophical intuitions within the Aristotelian framework, which, among its other good points, had the advantage of being currently used and at everyone's disposal. He so well succeeded in making the Aristotelian method his own, that his philosophy has been called a Christian Aristotelianism. Its novelty, when compared to St. Thomas', would simply consist in the absorption of a larger amount of Augustinianism.

Personally, I do not share this view, which has been expressed by the French Scotist, Father Belmond.* Likewise, I consider as very questionable the opinion of Father Veuthey, who charges that Duns Scotus lets Aristotle gain the upper hand, and that he thus betrays the Augustinian inspiration, which

---

* Cf. Séraphin Belmond, "Simples remarques sur l'idéologie comparée de saint Thomas et de Duns Scot," *Revue de philosophie,* 14, vol. XXIV (1914), 242-60; *idem,* "Essai de synthèse philosophique du scotisme," *La France Franciscaine,* XVI (1933), 73-131. *(Tr.)*

nevertheless can be traced here and there in his system.* For me Duns Scotus remains an Augustinian who profited to the utmost degree by the Aristotelian method in the exposition of the thoughts and doctrines that form his metaphysical vision of reality. Thus, even from this viewpoint, Duns Scotus appears to be a serious and constructive thinker, deeply penetrated with a sense of tradition, which at the time was not merely Franciscan but rather Catholic. At the same time, he keeps his mind open to progress and cultural development and profits by them, convinced that he will thus be a faithful servant of the truth.

---

* Cf. Léon Veuthey, "Augustinismus und Aristotelismus. Eine Erwiderung auf: Firmin Hohmann, O.F.M.: Ist Duns Skotus Augustinist oder Aristoteliker?" *Wissenschaft und Weisheit*, IV (1937), 211-15. *(Tr.)*

II

DUNS SCOTUS AND THE FUTURE

Having seen Dun Scotus' position in the past, let us now look at the importance and the prospects of the Scotistic heritage for the future.

The history of Scotism has not yet been written. It is still in the preparatory phase, as this or that Scotistic figure is chosen as the object of a particular study, or this or that Scotistic doctrine is considered in its evolution and set in relation to other doctrines. This is not the place to mention even briefly the main contributions that modern Scotistic literature can offer to a researcher. While an expert in the field is no doubt acquainted with them, to the ordinary reader they would be of no interest. It is an indisputable fact, however, that along with the Thomistic school, a Scotistic school of thought has emerged and flourished. Throughout the centuries it has given to the Church a great number of first-class theologians, saintly preachers, and formidable defenders of the faith. The number of philosophical and theological works written in the name of Scotus during the centuries is imposing, for they are counted by the hundreds.[2]

---

[2] Cf. Uriel Smeets, O.F.M., *Lineamenta bibliographiae scotisticae* (Rome: Typographia Augustiniana, 1942).

Duns Scotus' influence upon modern nonscholastic philosophers is almost nil. This is due to the fact that very few among them have had a direct knowledge of scholasticism. Father Scaramuzzi has pointed out certain important parallels between the thought of Duns Scotus and that of Giambattista Vico.* It is also an undeniable fact that some modern historians, like Windelband, have noticed a certain speculative affinity between Scotistic doctrines and various doctrines of Leibniz.** It would be of great historical interest to study the extent to which Rosmini was inspired by Duns Scotus, whom he knows and quotes with great respect in working out his doctrine of the idea of being.

Some historians have considerably exaggerated Duns Scotus' influence upon the nominalistic movement. They have gone so far as to affirm that Ockham merely draws natural conclusions from Scotistic doctrines. This historical thesis has met with some favor. However, the best medieval historians of today, when they do not reject this thesis entirely, raise at least some doubt as to its foundation. It is beyond question that some Scotistic doctrines taken out of context, such as the doctrine of "haecceity" and the doctrine concerning the knowability of the singular, which is closely related to it, could have been exploited by the nominalists. But it is one thing to admit this,

---

* Cf. Diomede Scaramuzzi, "Le infiltrazioni della dottrina di Giovanni Duns Scoto in Giambattista Vico," *Studi Francescani,* 23, vol. XII (1926), 149-70. *(Tr.)*

** Cf. Wilhelm Windelband, *A History of Philosophy,* trans. by James H. Tufts (New York: Harper & Brothers, 1958), II, 420-25. Concerning the relationship between Leibniz and Duns Scotus, whom he calls "the most important thinker of the Christian Middle Ages" (*ibid.,* I, 314), Windelband observes: "The relations of Leibniz to the greatest of the Scholastics are to be recognized not only in this point [the hypothetical necessity or contingency of the world], but also in many others; though as yet they have unfortunately not found the consideration or treatment that they deserve." *Ibid.,* II, 425, n. 1. *(Tr.)*

and an entirely different thing to affirm that Scotistic philosophy necessarily prepares the way for nominalism. Otherwise, any great thinker could be held responsible for the more or less indirect paternity of all later philosophies claiming dependence on him or on some of his doctrines. The fact that Ockham was a Franciscan, and had probably been a disciple of Duns Scotus,* does not in itself constitute any solid ground for the assertion that his system depends on Duns Scotus' doctrine. The history of philosophy teaches us that a thinker's most formidable rival usually emerges from his school. Shall we say that Duns Scotus paves the way to nominalism precisely because nominalism is the natural outcome of opposition to his philosophy? In this case, we definitely commit ourselves to an abuse of terms. One philosophical movement prepares the way for another only when this latter is a logical outgrowth of the former.

In Catholic cultural circles not only is Duns Scotus set aside and neglected, but he is often looked upon with suspicion as though he were an insidious forerunner of heresy. This attitude might perhaps be conceivable in regard to certain Catholic thinkers, like Rosmini, for example. A strong support of such an attitude is found in the fact that the Church has condemned forty doctrinal propositions attributed—whether rightly or wrongly, it is not for us to decide—to the philosopher of Rovereto. However, it is difficult to understand how this same attitude could have become traditional in regard to Duns Scotus. There is not a single document of the Church that

---

* We have no definite data concerning Ockham's early life and studies. On the basis of a recently discovered document, he would have been ordained sub-deacon on February 26, 1306, i.e., two years before Scotus' death. Perhaps he heard Scotus' lectures. Most probably he pursued his higher studies in theology at Oxford from about 1309 to 1315. Cf. *Ockham: Philosophical Writings*. A selection edited and translated by Philotheus Boehner, O.F.M. (Edinburgh-New York: Nelson, 1957), Introduction, pp. xi-xii. *(Tr.)*

either directly or indirectly puts the Catholic scholars on their guard against any error or possible danger in the Scotistic speculation. Quite the opposite! There are authoritative acts and statements showing that the Church has always held Duns Scotus' works in high esteem. This is true in the first place of his theology, but it can be said to be equally true of his philosophy, which in him, as in any other scholastic, is intimately connected with theological doctrine. Here are some of these acts and statements.

Eminent Scotists have been raised to high posts in the Catholic Church, such as Cardinal Lorenzo Brancati and Cardinal Sarnano, and even to the Supreme Pontificate, such as Pope Sixtus IV, Pope Sixtus V, and Pope Clement XIV. In the citation written on the occasion of Cardinal Sarnano's appointment, Pope Sixtus V stated among other things: "You have devoted your remarkable, industrious activity to restoring to their integrity many volumes of Duns Scotus and other pious writers, which had been corrupted through misprints. For this reason and many others known to Us personally, We are sure you will be very useful to Us and greatly contribute to the welfare of the Roman Church."[3] Evidently, in Pope Sixtus V's view, the zeal shown by Sarnano in making Duns Scotus' doctrine known is not something worthy of blame; rather it is something that deserves praise, for it fits him to be called to higher posts and greater enterprises for the good of the Church.

Many works written by Scotistic scholars have been dedicated to popes, who never failed to show their appreciation to the authors. To Father Ferdinando Garcia, who had presented Pope Pius X with his *Mentis in Deum quotidiana elevatio duce B. Joanne Duns Scoto,* Cardinal Merry del Val wrote: "His Holiness has been very pleased with your book. He found it

---

[3] Willibrordus Lampen, *B. J. Duns Scotus et Sancta Sedes* (Quaracchi: Typographia Collegii S. Bonaventurae, 1929), p. 20.

very interesting and particularly useful for clerics and semi-narians." To the same Father, following the publication of the first volumes of the *Opus Oxoniense,* Cardinal Gasparri wrote: "Your volumes have been received by the Holy Father with the greatest pleasure. Duns Scotus is a thinker who discusses most profound matters so acutely and abundantly that the reader will readily admit that this holy man has been cherished by wisdom as by a loving mother."[4]

Furthermore, it has been historically ascertained that a decree of the Sacred Congregation of Cardinals was issued during the Pontificate of Pope Paul V, instructing the Master of the Sacred Palace that "anything that is proved to be the work of Duns Scotus may be printed without further examination."[5]

The Holy See has clearly manifested its thought with regard to Scotus by approving throughout the centuries the General Constitutions of the Friars Minor, which formerly imposed on the Professors of the Order adherence to Duns Scotus' doctrines in their teaching. The present Constitutions are more liberal, and prescribe only that "in the philosophical and theological faculties the Lectors shall earnestly endeavor to follow the Franciscan School; they shall hold in high regard the other Scholastics, especially the Angelic Doctor, St. Thomas, the Heavenly Patron of Catholic Schools."[6] However, the Ordinations of Toledo, approved by Pope Urban VIII on October 31, 1634, in the brief *Ad Eximios,* prescribed categorically and with a rigor that has been since abandoned because of its incompatibility with the Franciscan largeness of spirit: "Whenever, either directly or indirectly, orally or by writing, the Lectors of philosophy and theology have deviated from Duns Scotus' doctrine, they are to be irrevocably deprived of their lectorate.

---

[4] *Ibid.,* p. 26.

[5] *Ibid.,* p. 27.

[6] *The Rule and General Constitutions of the Order of Friars Minor* (Rome: The General Curia of the Order, 1953), p. 100, art. 238, n. 6.

And in order that uniformity in the philosophical doctrines of our most Subtle Doctor be preserved, as far as possible, in our Order, the Most Reverend Father General will at the earliest opportunity entrust at least four Fathers who hold a doctorate with the task of preparing a manual of disciplines according to Scotus' thought, which shall be followed in the future by the Lectors of philosophy."[7] It is evident that if from the Catholic viewpoint Duns Scotus' doctrine were even in the least suspicious or dangerous, the Holy See could not officially approve such dispositions.

That Scotistic teaching was received freely and without prejudice in large circles of Christian scholars is sufficiently demonstrated by the fact that a Scotistic chair existed at one time in all universities and theological faculties in Italy, France, England, Poland, Spain, Latin America, and even at Kiev in Russia.[8] Things went so well with the Scotistic school, that in the seventeenth century Caramuel, a professor of Louvain, could make the forthright statement: "The Scotistic school is more numerous than all other schools taken together."[9]

Has the Church's mind changed since those times? It may seem so. There are many, in fact, who believe that a great change has taken place in Church discipline since the publication of the encyclical *Aeterni Patris,* Pope Pius X's "motu proprio" *Doctoris Angelici,* and the twenty-four theses of the Sacred Congregation of Studies on March 7, 1916. These are all documents to be considered in order to evaluate properly the prescriptions of Canon Law, nn. 589 and 1366. A Catholic, they claim, who desires to abide, as is his duty, by Church

[7] Lampen, *op. cit.,* p. 30.

[8] Cf. Ephrem Longpré, *La Philosophie du B. Duns Scot, op. cit.,* pp. 10-12.

[9] *Ibid.,* p. 9. [The statement "Scoti schola numerosior est omnibus aliis simul sumptis" is discussed by Felix Bak, O.F.M. Conv., in *Franciscan Studies,* XVI (1956), 144-65. *(Tr.)*]

directives, can no longer deviate in any way from the speculative line traced by St. Thomas; nor can he give any consideration to doctrines in contrast with the Thomistic principles.

I do not dare to make any statement concerning the meaning and value of these directives of the Church, nor do I wish
to suggest any interpretation that may sound presumptuous.
I will leave the word to Cardinal Franz Ehrle, who discusses
this problem expressly and with authority.[10] The conclusion of
his discussion follows:

> Wishing to summarize the results of our discussion, we
> must say that the Church has been very wise in so earn-
> estly commending scholastic philosophy and theology to
> her schools and men of learning, as well as in prescribing
> it for ecclesiastical institutes. For everyone, even if of a
> different faith but free from prejudice, can readily see
> the hand of divine Providence in the development of
> this philosophy. Because of their metaphysical founda-
> tions, their method, and their harmony with revelation,
> scholastic philosophy and scholastic theology alone—this
> latter being intimately connected with the former—can
> demonstrate and develop the prerequisites of revelation.
> They are also their best commentary and defense,
> since they make them part of a definite and unified sys-
> tem. One will also readily understand why the Popes, espe-
> cially in this century, place so much emphasis on the
> study of St. Thomas and his doctrine. The times are too
> difficult to allow us to spend our best energies in mere
> scholastic disputes and controversies. There will no doubt
> always be discrepancies of opinion and controversies which
> need be discussed in a scientific manner. However, in

[10] Card. Franz Ehrle, *La scolastica e i suoi compiti odierni* (Turin:
S.E.I., 1935). [See also Franz Pelster, "The Authority of St. Thomas
in Catholic Schools and the Sacred Sciences," *Franciscan Studies,*
XIII, n. 4 (Dec., 1953), 1-26; and Claude Mindorff, "A Common Sense
View of the 24 Theses," *American Ecclesiastical Review,* LXX (1924),
531-33. *(Tr.)*]

this case the real meaning of the problems is the decisive factor, not tradition or the desire of this or that particular school to predominate. It is in view of this fact that the Church has designed St. Thomas as the common Master. Following his example, we must discuss the great problems in such a way that truth will always prevail, not this or that particular scholastic tradition. In this common and unbiased search for truth St. Thomas is really a wonderful example. For he not only showed us the way, but he also gave us the means and laid down the foundations for the solution of many problems.

Finally, let us fully appreciate the fact that, despite the high esteem in which she holds the Common Doctor, the Church refuses to stress the saint's doctrine in such wise that the opinions of other important schools may appear to be condemned or in any way underrated. She knows only too well the importance of free competition of ideas in the search for truth, for it alone makes possible the complete clarification of a problem, even though starting points may be different. As long as faith and love are preserved, such competition will only benefit the truth and the Church herself, which is the protector of all truth. This is why she grants the *iusta libertas* to all teachers, students, and researchers. If an individual scholar, an institute, or a religious order wants to adhere more strictly to St. Thomas or to another Master, they have full right and freedom to do so.[11]

These are such precious words that they well justify the length of the quotation. These words should be engraved upon certain Catholic schools and institutes, where courses are given quite freely on Plato, Leibniz, and Kant, while the objective exposition, or the mere mentioning of a doctrine of St. Bonaventure or Duns Scotus, let alone of Rosmini or Blondel, is considered an attack on the integrity of the faith

[11] *Ibid.*, pp. 91-92. [Cf. Allocution (Oct. 17, 1953) of Pius XII to the Gregorianum, in *Acta Apostolicae Sedis*, XLVI (1953), 682-90; cited in part in *Franciscan Studies*, XIV (1954), 204-209. *(Tr.)*]

and the peace of conscience. This is certainly not in conformity with the directives of the Church, for which the return to St. Thomas "means in the first place the return to his doctrine, and in the second place, and even more, the return to his spirit and his method of work."[12] The Church prescribes the study of the *Summa Theologiae* in the schools, not because she wants to impose upon us as a dogma the doctrines therein contained, but because the *Summa Theologiae* is "the most concise synthesis" of "scholastic doctrines, and most suitable for the schools."[13]

These pages have not been intended to be a complete or documented exposition of the Scotistic thought, but if they eventually lead their reader to a more objective and conscientious study of Duns Scotus, they have attained their purpose. They may at the same time represent a first attempt to insure greater comprehension of the Scotistic doctrine and to counteract the groundless charges of which Duns Scotus has been and still is the unfortunate victim.

---

[12] *Ibid.,* p. 57.
[13] *Ibid.,* p. 72.

SELECTED BIBLIOGRAPHY*

PRIMARY SOURCES

A. DUNS SCOTUS' WORKS

Scotus, John Duns. *Opera Omnia*. 12 vols. Ed. Luke Wadding. Lyons, 1639.

————. *Opera Omnia*. Editio nova iuxta editionem Waddingi. 26 vols. Paris: Vivès, 1891-1895.

————. *Opera Omnia,* studio et cura Commissionis Scotisticae ad fidem codicum edita. 5 vols. of the *Ordinatio* published. Civitas Vaticana: Typis polyglottis Vaticanis, 1950-.

————. *Commentaria Oxoniensia.* 2 vols. Ed. Marianus Fernandez García. Quaracchi: Typographia Collegii S. Bonaventurae, 1912-1914.

————. *De Primo Principio.* A Revised Text and a Translation by Evan Roche. St. Bonaventure, N. Y.: The Franciscan Institute, 1949.

————. *Obras del Doctor Sutil Juan Duns Escoto.* Latin text and Spanish translation from the Vatican critical edition of Duns Scotus' *Opera Omnia.* Vol. I: *Dios Uno y Trino.* Madrid: Biblioteca de Autores Cristianos, 1960. Other volumes to follow.

B. COLLECTIONS OF TEXTS

Déodat, Marie de Basly. *Capitalia Opera Beati J. Duns Scoti.* 2 vols. Le Havre: La Bonne Parole, 1908-1911.

Frassen, Claudius. *Scotus Academicus.* 12 vols. New edition by Marianus Fernandez García and Cyprianus Paolini. Rome: Typographia Sallustiana, 1900-1902.

---

* This bibliography has been greatly enlarged and brought up to date. *(Tr.)*

Hieronymus de Montefortino. *Ioannis Duns Scoti Summa Theo-logica.* 6 vols. New edition by Marianus Fernandez García and Cyprianus Paolini. Rome: Typographia Sallustiana, 1900-1903.

Minges, Parthenius. *Ioannis Duns Scoti Doctrina Philosophica et Theologica.* 2 vols. Quaracchi: Typographia Collegii S. Bonaventurae, 1930.

Scaramuzzi, Diomede. *Duns Scoto. Summula.* Ed. "Testi Cristiani." Florence: Libreria Editrice Fiorentina, 1932.

SECONDARY SOURCES

A. GENERAL STUDIES

Balic, Carlo. "Circa positiones fundamentales Ioannis Duns Scoti," *Antonianum,* XXVIII (1953), 261-306.

———. "Duns Scoto, Giovanni," *Enciclopedia Cattolica.* Vol. IV, cols. 1982-1990.

———. "Giovanni Duns Scoto," *Grande Antologia Filosofica.* Ed. Istituto per la collaborazione culturale. Florence: Sansoni, 1957. Vol. IV, 1335-1354.

———. "Wadding, the Scotist," in *Father Luke Wadding. Commemorative Volume.* Dublin: Conmore and Reynold, 1957. Pp. 463-507. (Important for evaluation of Wadding's edition of Duns Scotus' *Opera Omnia.*)

Belmond, Séraphin. "Simples remarques sur l'idéologie comparée de saint Thomas et de Duns Scot," *Revue de philosophie,* 14, vol. XXIV (1914), 242-60.

———. "Essai de synthèse philosophique du scotisme," *La France Franciscaine,* XVI (1933), 73-131.

Béraud de Saint-Maurice. *John Duns Scotus. A Teacher for Our Times.* Trans. by Columban Duffy. St. Bonaventure, N. Y.: The Franciscan Institute, 1955.

Bettoni, Efrem. "Scoto, Giovanni Duns," *Enciclopedia Filosofica.* Ed. Istituto per la collaborazione culturale. Florence: Sansoni, 1957. Vol. IV, cols. 463-72.

Boehner, Philotheus. *The History of the Franciscan School,* Part III, *Duns Scotus* (manuscript). St. Bonaventure, N. Y.: The Franciscan Institute, 1945. Re-mimeographed at Duns Scotus College, Detroit, 1946.

———. "Scotus' Teaching according to Ockham," *Franciscan Studies,* VI (1946), 100-107; 362-75.

Copleston, Frederick. *A History of Philosophy.* Westminster: The Newman Press, 1950. Vol. II, pp. 476-551.

Déodat, Marie de Basly. *Scotus Docens. La construction doctrinale du B. Docteur subtil.* Le Havre: La Bonne Parole, 1934.

Fernandez García, Mariano. *Lexicon scholasticum philosophico-theologicum.* Quaracchi: Typographia Collegii S. Bonaventurae, 1906-1910.

Galikowski, Antonius M. "De praecipuis controversiis philosophico-theologicis inter thomistas et scotistas," *Collectanea Franciscana Slavica,* I (1937), 55-80.

Gilson, Étienne. "Avicenne et le point de départ de Duns Scot," *Archives d'histoire doctrinale et littéraire du Moyen-Âge,* II (1927), 89-149.

————. "Les seize premiers Theoremata et la pensée de Duns Scot," *Archives d'histoire doctrinale et littéraire du Moyen-Âge,* XII-XIII (1937-1938), 5-86.

————. *Jean Duns Scot. Introduction à ses positions fondamentales.* Paris: Vrin, 1952.

————. *History of Christian Philosophy in the Middle Ages.* New York: Random House, 1955. Pp. 454-64.

Harris, Charles R. S. *Duns Scotus.* 2 vols. Oxford: Clarendon Press, 1927.

Hohmann, Firmin. "Ist Duns Skotus Augustinist oder Aristoteliker?," *Wissenschaft und Weisheit,* IV (1937), 131-40.

Landry, Bernard. *Duns Scot.* Paris: Alcan, 1922.

Longpré, Ephrem. *La philosophie du B. Duns Scot.* Paris: Société et Librairie St. François d'Assise, 1924.

Maquart, François-Xavier. "Faut-il reviser les jugements des thomistes concernant la doctrine de Scot? Quelques thèses de l'intellectualisme scotiste," *Revue de philosophie,* 34, vol. IV (1934), 400-35.

Meyer, Fulgence. "John Duns Scot," *The Ecclesiastical Review,* LIII (1918), 632-50.

Minges, Parthenius. "Ioannes Duns Scotus," *The Franciscan Educational Conference,* III, pp. 49-64.

O'Neil, Albert M. "Le bienheureux Jean Duns Scot en face de saint Thomas d'Aquin," *La France Franciscaine,* VIII (1925), 491-501.

Pelzer, Auguste. "A propos de Jean Duns Scot et des études scotistes," *Revue néoscolastique de philosophie,* XXV (1923), 410-20.

Porcelloni, Ambrogio. "L'intellettualismo di Duns Scoto alla luce della nuova edizione," *Rivista di filosofia neoscolastica,* XLIV (1952), 192-212.

Prado, Norberto del. "Escoto y Santo Tomás," *Ciencia Tomista,* V (1914-15), n. 28, pp. 28-45; n. 49, pp. 196-222.

Raymond de Courcerault. "La philosophie critique de Duns Scot et le criticisme de Kant," *Études Franciscaines,* XXII (1909), 669-87.

Schmalz, Gerard. "The Philosophy of Duns Scotus," *The Franciscan Educational Conference,* III (1921), 89-106.

Sharp, Dorothea E. *Franciscan Philosophy at Oxford in the XIII Century.* London: Oxford University Press, 1930.

Thonnard, F. J. *A Short History of Philosophy.* Trans. by Edward A. Maziarz, Paris: Desclée, 1955. Pp. 434-52.

Vacant, Jean-Michel-Alfred. *Études comparées sur la philosophie de S. Thomas d'Aquin et sur celle de Duns Scot.* Paris-Lyons, 1891.

Varesio, Carolus F. de. *Promptuarium scoticum.* 2 vols. Venice: Andrea Poleti, 1690.

Vyskocil, Capistranus. "Brevis conspectus doctrinae philosophicae ac theologicae Ioannis Duns Scoti," *Collectanea Franciscana Slavica,* I (1937), 360-91.

Woestyne, Zacharias van de. *Scholae Franciscanae aptatus cursus philosophicus.* 2 vols. Malines: Typographia S. Francisci, 1921-1925. New edition of vol. I in 2 smaller volumes. *Ibid.,* 1932-1933.

Wulf, Maurice de. *History of Mediaeval Philosophy.* Trans. by Ernest C. Messenger. London-New York: Longmans, Green and Co., 1926. Vol. II, pp. 69-90.

B. SPECIAL STUDIES

Biography

Bertoni, Alexandre. *Le B. Jean Duns Scot, sa vie, ses doctrines, ses disciples.* Levanto: Tipografia dell'Immacolata, 1917.

Callebaut, André. "A propos du B. Duns Scot de Littledean," *Archivum Franciscanum Historicum,* XXIV (1931), 305-29.

Giusto, Egidio M. *Vita del B. Giovanni Duns Scoto.* Assisi: Tipografia industriale, 1921.

Little, Andrew G. "Chronological Notes on the Life of Duns Scotus," *English Historical Review,* XLVII (1932), 568-82.

Pelster, Franz. "Handschriftliches zu Skotus mit neuen Angaben über sein Leben," *Franziskanische Studien,* X (1923), 1-32.

Bibliography

Balic, Carolus. *Relatio a commissione scotistica exhibita capitulo generali Fratrum Minorum Assisii A. D. 1939 celebrato.* Rome: Schola typographica "Pio X," 1939.

Bettoni, Efrem. *Vent'anni di studi scotisti* (1920-1940). Milan: "Rivista di filosofia neoscolastica," 1943.

Commissio Scotistica. "De Ordinatione I. D. Scoti disquisitio historico-critica," in *Opera Omnia*. Vatican Edition. Rome, 1950. Vol. I, pp. 9*-299*.

Grajewski, Maurice J. "Scotistic Bibliography of the Last Decade (1929-1939)," *Franciscan Studies,* I (1941), n. 1, pp. 73-78; n. 2, pp. 55-72; n. 3, pp. 71-76; II (1942), 61-71; 158-73.

―――――. "Duns Scotus in the Light of Modern Research," in *Proceedings of the American Catholic Philosophical Association,* XVIII (1942), 168-85.

Huallachain, C. O. "On Recent Studies of the Opening Question in Scotus's *Ordinatio*," *Franciscan Studies,* XV (1955), 1-29.

McGregor, M. B. *Sources and Literature of Scot.* Glasgow: Callum, 1934.

Schaefer, Odulfus. *Bibliographia de vita, operibus et doctrina Iohannis Duns Scoti, Doctoris Subtilis ac Mariani, saec. XIX-XX.* Rome: Herder, 1955.

Smeets, Uriel. *Lineamenta bibliographiae scotisticae.* Rome: Typographia Augustiniana, 1942. It includes the Scotistic bibliography from the 15th to the 20th century.

Logic and Epistemology

Barth, Timotheus. "Duns Skotus und die ontologische Grundlage unserer Verstandeserkenntnis," *Franziskanische Studien,* XXXIII (1951), 348-84.

Belmond, Séraphin. "L'intellect actif d'après Jean Duns Scot," *Revue de philosophie,* 30, vol. I (1930), 31-54.

―――――. "Essai sur la théorie de la connaissance d'après Jean Duns Scot," *La France Franciscaine,* XVIII (1935), 5-32; 197-234.

Bérubé, Camille. "La connaissance intellectuelle du singulier matériel chez Duns Scot," *Franciscan Studies,* XIII (March, 1953), 29-49; (Dec., 1953), 27-58. (To be continued.)

Bettoni, Efrem. *Dalla dottrina degli universali alla teoria della conoscenza in Duns Scoto.* Florence: Vallecchi, 1941.

Carreras y Artau, Joaquín. "La doctrina de los universales en Juan Scot. Una contribución a la historia de la lógica en el siglo XIII," *Archivo Ibero-Americano,* XXXIV (1931), 5-29; 209-33.

Day, Sebastian J. *Intuitive Cognition. A Key to the Significance of the Later Scholastics.* St. Bonaventure, N. Y.: The Franciscan Institute, 1947. Pp. 39-139.

Heiser, Basil. "The *primum cognitum* according to Duns Scotus," *Franciscan Studies,* II (1942), 193-216.

Klug, Hubert. "Die sinnliche Erkenntnis nach dem seligen Johannes Duns Skotus," *Franziskanische Studien,* XI (1924), 237-57.

Martínez, Juan M. "Criteriologia escotista. Doctrina textual del B. J. Duns Escoto," *Verdad y Vida,* III (1945), 651-81; IV (1946), 63-85.

Messner, Reinhold. *Schauendes und begriffliches Erkennen nach Duns Skotus.* Freiburg in Br.: Herder, 1942.

Picard, Novatus. "De positione problematis cognitionis apud Duns Scotum ac de eius ratione obiectiva," *Antonianum,* XIX (1944), 283-309.

Raymond de Courcerault. "La théorie de l'induction. Duns Scot, précurseur de Bacon," *Études Franciscaines,* XXI (1909), 113-26; 270-79.

Soleri, G. "Studi scotisti di gnoseologia e di teodicea," *Sapienza* (1956), 70-83; 205-21.

Swiezawski, Stefan. "Les intentions premières et les intentions secondes chez Jean Duns Scot," *Archives d'histoire doctrinale et littéraire du Moyen-Âge,* IX (1934), 205-60.

Tochowics, Paulus. *Joannis Duns Scoti de cognitionis doctrina.* "Studia Friburgensia." Paderbon: Bonifacius Drückerei, 1926.

Vacant, Jean-Michel-Alfred. "La théorie de la connaissance selon S. Thomas et selon Duns Scot," *Annales de philosophie chrétienne,* XXI (1889-90), 5-30; 185-201; 210-25; 321-44.

Veuthey, Léon. "L'intuition scotiste et le sens du concret," *Études Franciscaines,* XLIX (1937), 76-91.

Vier, Peter C. *Evidence and Its Function According to John Duns Scotus.* St. Bonaventure, N. Y.: The Franciscan Institute, 1951.

Werner, Carl. *Die Psychologie und Erkenntnislehre des Duns Scotus.* "Denskschrift Akad. Wissenschaft," vol. 26. Wien, 1877, pp. 345-438.

Zuccherelli, Donato. "La cognizione nel pensiero del B. G. Duns Scoto," *Studi Francescani,* 12, vol. I (1914-15), 1-15.

————. "Il problema criteriologico nel pensiero del B. Giovanni Duns Scoto," *Studi Francescani,* 12, vol. I (1914-15), 201-11.

Metaphysics

Barth, Timotheus. "De fundamento univocationis apud Ioannem Duns Scotum," *Antonianum,* XIV (1939), 181-206; 277-98; 373-92.

————. "De argumentis et univocationis entis natura apud Joannem Duns Scotum," *Collectanea Franciscana,* XIV (1944), 5-56.

————. "De univocationis scotisticae intentione principali necnon valore critico," *Antonianum,* XXVIII (1953), 72-110.

————. "Individualität und Allgemeinheit bei Johan Duns Scotus," *Wissenschaft und Weisheit,* XVI (1953), 191-213.

Belmond, Séraphin. "L'être transcendant d'après Duns Scot," *Revue de philosophie, 9,* vol. XIV (1909), 67-87.

————. "L'essenza e l'esistenza secondo Duns Scoto," *Rivista di filosofia neoscolastica,* II (1910), 281-89.

————. "L'univocité scotiste: Ses fondements," *Revue de philosophie,* 13, vol. XXII (1913), 137-56.

————. "L'heccéisme scotiste," *Études Franciscaines,* XLVII (1935), 159-70.

Chiocchetti, Emilio. "L'univocità dell'essere in Dio e nelle creature," *Sophia,* X (1942), 195-206.

Costa, Ersilio. "L'essenza del reale in Duns Scoto," *Ricerche religiose,* V (1929), 412-28; VII (1931), 227-41.

Gilson, Étienne. "Metaphysik und Theologie nach Scotus," *Franziskanische Studien,* XXII (1935), 209-31.

————. "L'objet de la métaphysique selon Duns Scot," *Mediaeval Studies,* X (1948), 21-92.

Grajewski, Maurice J. *The Formal Distinction of Duns Scotus.* Washington, D. C.: The Catholic University of America Press, 1944.

Hayen, André. "L'être et la personne selon le bienheureux Duns Scot," *Revue philosophique de Louvain,* LIII (1955), 525-41.

Heiser, Basil. "The Metaphysics of Duns Scotus," *Franciscan Studies,* II (1942), 379-96.

Kraus, Johannes. *Die Lehre des Johannes Duns Skotus von der "natura communis."* Studia Friburgensia. Paderborn: Bonifacius-Drückerei, 1927.

Lemieux, Béraud de Saint-Maurice. "Existential Import in the Philosophy of Duns Scotus," *Franciscan Studies,* IX (1949), 274-313.

MacDonagh, Hilaire. "La notion d'être dans la métaphysique de Jean Duns Scot," *Revue néoscolastique de philosophie,* XXX (1928), 400-17; XXXI (1929), 81-96; 148-81.

Messner, Reinhold. "Das Individuationsprinzip in skotistischer Schau," *Wissenschaft und Weisheit,* I (1934), 8-27.

Minges, Parthenius. "Beitrag zur Lehre des Duns Scotus über die Univokation des Seinsbegriffes," *Philosophisches Jahrbuch,* XX (1907), 306-23.

————. *Der angebliche excessive Realismus des Duns Scotus.* Münster i. W.: Aschendorffsche Buchhandlung, 1908.

Muehlen, Heribert. *Sein und Person nach Johannes Duns Scotus.* Werl in W.: Dietrich-Coelde, 1954.

Oromí, Miguel. "Duns Escoto y el objeto de la Metafísica," in *Métodos y Principios Filosóficos*. Madrid: Editorial Cisneros, 1960. Pp. 269-312.

————. "El ser y la existencia de Dios en Escoto," in *Métodos y Principios Filosóficos*. Madrid: Editorial Cisneros, 1960. Pp. 315-29.

Rosenberg, Jean Randall. *The Principle of Individuation. A Comparative Study of St. Thomas, Scotus and Suarez*. Ph.D. Thesis. Washington, D. C.: The Catholic University of America Press, 1950.

Sciacca, Michele Federico. *La "Haecceitas" di Duns Scoto*. Studi sulla filosofia medioevale e moderna. Naples: Perella, 1935.

Shircel, Cyril L. *The Univocity of the Concept of Being in the Philosophy of Duns Scotus*. Washington, D. C.: The Catholic University of America Press, 1942.

Sotiello, Gabriel de. "El punto de partida de la metafísica de Duns Scotus," *Naturaleza y Gracia*, I (1954), 85-103.

Wolter, Allan B. *The Transcendentals and Their Function in the Metaphysics of Duns Scotus*. Washington, D. C.: The Catholic University of America Press, 1946.

————. *Summula Metaphysicae*. Milwaukee: Bruce, 1958.

Cosmology

Albanese, Cornelio. "Della natura del tempo secondo il venerabile Dottor sottile e mariano," *Studi Francescani*, 12, vol. I (1914-1915), 465-85.

Baudoux, Bernard. "De forma corporeitatis scotistica," *Antonianum*, XIII (1938), 429-74.

Bettoni, Efrem. "Duns Scoto e l'argomento del moto," *Rivista di filosofia neoscolastica*, XXXIII (1941), 477-89.

Borgmann, Pacificus. "Die Stellungnahme des Duns Scotus zum aristotelisch-thomistischen Bewegungsgesetz: *Quidquid movetur ab alio movetur*," *Wissenschaft und Weisheit*, IV (1937), 36-42.

Campbell, Bertrand J. *The Problem of One or Plural Substantial Forms in Man as Found in the Works of St. Thomas Aquinas and John Duns Scotus*. Paterson, N. J.: St. Anthony Guild Press, 1940.

Chiriotti, Edilio. "Il concetto di materia in Duns Scoto," *Giornale critico della filosofia italiana*, XI (1930), 113-34.

Klug, Hubert, "Die Lehre des Johannes Duns Skotus über die Materie und Form nach den Quellen dargestellt," *Philosophisches Jahrbuch*, XXX (1917), 44-78.

Stella, Prospero. *L'ilemorfismo di Giovanni Duns Scoto.* Turin: Società Editrice Internazionale, 1956.

Vogt, Berard. "The *forma corporeitatis* of Duns Scotus and Modern Science," *Franciscan Studies,* 24, vol. III (1943), 47-62.

Psychology

Auer, Johan. *Die menschliche Willensfreiheit im Lehrsystem des Thomas von Aquin und Johannes Duns Scotus.* Munich: Hueber, 1938.

Belmond, Séraphin. "Prétendu anti-intellectualisme du Docteur subtil," *Études Franciscaines,* XXXI (1914), 561-73; XXXII (1914), 5-20.

————. "Le rôle de la volonté dans la philosophie de Duns Scot," *Études Franciscaines,* XLIX (1937), 650-59.

Carreras y Artau, Joaquín. *Ensayo sobre el voluntarismo de J. Duns Scoto.* Gerona: Tipografía Carreras, 1923.

Chauvet, Fidel. *Las pasiones. Las ideas filosóficas de J. Duns Escoto sobre las pasiones.* Barcelona: Beltram, 1936.

Chiocchetti, Emilio. "Il volontarismo di G. Duns Scoto," *Studi Francescani,* XII, Ser. 3 (1940), 232-39.

Cresi, Angelo. "La posizione di Scoto nella questione dell'immortalità dell'anima," *La Verna,* XI (1913-14), 49-65.

Cresswell, J. R. "Duns Scotus on the Will," *Franciscan Studies,* XIII (June-Sept., 1953), 147-58.

Fioravanti, Agostino. "La distinzione tra l'anima e le sue facoltà nella dottrina del ven. Duns Scoto," *Studi Francescani,* 12, vol. I (1914-15), 235-44.

Gilson, Étienne. "Wille und Sittlichkeit nach Johannes Duns Skotus," *Wissenschaft und Weisheit,* I (1958), 9-17.

Klug, Hubert. "Die Lehre des seligen Johannes Duns Skotus über die Seele," *Philosophisches Jahrbuch,* XXXVI (1923), 131-45; 198-212; XXXVII (1924), 57-75.

————. "L'activité appétitive de l'âme d'après le bienheureux Duns Scot," *Études Franciscaines,* XXXVII (1925), 532-42; XXXVIII (1926), 78-97; 270-92; 564-93.

————. "L'activité intellectuelle selon le bienheureux Duns Scot," *Études Franciscaines,* XLI (1929), 5-23; 113-30; 244-69; 381-91; 517-38; XLII (1930), 129-45.

Léandre de Sesma. "La volonté dans la philosophie de J. Duns Scot," *Estudios Franciscanos,* 21, vol. XXXIX (1927), 220-49; 572-93.

Libertini, C. *Intelletto e volontà in Tommaso e Duns Scoto.* Naples: Perella, 1926.

210 *Duns Scotus*

Longpré, Ephrem. "The Psychology of Duns Scot and its Modernity," *The Franciscan Educational Conference*, XIII (1931), 19-77.

Minges, Parthenius. *Ist Duns Scotus Indeterminist?* Münster in W.: Aschendorffsche Veragsbuchhandlung, 1905.

Piana, Celestino. "La controversia della distinzione fra anima e potenze," *Miscellanea, Centro studi medievali*, I (1956), 65-168.

Ryan, John K. *The Doctrine of John Duns Scotus on the Nature and Value of the Rational Arguments for Immortality*. M.A. Thesis. Washington, D. C.: The Catholic University of America Press, 1931.

Siebeck, H. "Die Willenslehre bei Johannes Duns Scotus," *Zeitschrift für Philosophie und philosophische Kritik*, XCII (1898), 179-216.

Vanni Rovighi, Sofia. "L'immortalità dell'anima nel pensiero di Giovanni Duns Scoto," *Rivista di filosofia neoscolastica*, XXIII (1931), 78-104.

Theodicy

Barth, Timotheus. "De tribus viis diversis existentiam divinam attingendi. Disquisitio historico-collativa inter s. Thomam, Henricum Gandavensem, Duns Scotum," *Antonianum*, XVIII (1943), 91-117.

Belmond, Séraphin. "L'existence de Dieu d'après Duns Scot," *Revue de philosophie*, 8, vol. XIII (1908), 241-68; 364-81.

————. "La connaissance de Dieu d'après Duns Scot," *Revue de philosophie*, 10, vol. XVII (1910), 496-514.

————. *Études sur la philosophie de Duns Scot. Dieu, existence et cognoscibilité*. Paris: Beauchesne, 1913.

Bettoni, Efrem. *L'ascesa a Dio in Duns Scoto*. Milan: "Vita e Pensiero," 1943.

————. *Il problema della conoscibilità di Dio nella scuola francescana*. Padua: Cedam, 1950.

————. "De argumentatione Doctoris Subtilis quoad existentiam Dei," *Antonianum*, XXVIII (1953), 39-58.

Borgmann, Pacificus. "Über die Stellung des Duns Scotus zum sog. ontologischen Gottesbeweis," *Lektorenkonferenz*, VI-VII, pp. 116-19.

Fackler, Franz P. *Der Seinsbegriff in seiner Bedeutung für die Gotteserkenntnis des Duns Scotus*. Friedberg-Augsburg: Baur, 1933.

Gilson, Étienne. "L'existence de Dieu selon Duns Scot," *Mediaeval Studies*, XI (1949), 23-61.

————. "Nature et portée des preuves scotistes de l'existence de Dieu," *Mélanges Joseph Maréchal*, II, pp. 378-95.

Klein, Joseph. *Der Gottesbegriff des Johannes Duns Scotus*. Paderborn: Schöningh, 1913.

Minges, Parthenius. *Der Gottesbegriff des Duns Skotus*. Vienna: Mayr, 1907.

————. *Das Verhältnis zwischen Glauben und Wissen, Theologie und Philosophie nach D. Scotus*. Paderborn: Schöningh, 1908.

Owens, Joseph. "The Special Characteristic of the Scotistic Proof that God Exists," *Analecta Gregoriana*, LXVII, Series Facultatis Philosophicae, Sect. A, n. 6 (1954), 311-27.

Puech, Léonard. "Duns Scot et l'argument de saint Anselme," *Nos cahiers*, II (1937), 183-99.

————. "Une preuve oubliée de l'existence de Dieu," *Nos cahiers*, IV (1939), 225-71.

Schwamm, Hermann. *Das göttliche Vorherwissen bei Duns Scotus und seinem ersten Anhängern*. Philosophie und Grenzwissenschaften, 5, 1-4. Innsbruck: Rauch, 1934.

Wolter, Allan B. "Duns Scotus on the Nature of Man's Knowledge of God," *Review of Metaphysics*, I, n. 2 (Dec., 1947), 3-36.

————. "The Theologism of Duns Scotus," *Franciscan Studies*, VII (1947), 257-73; 367-98.

————. "Duns Scotus on the Natural Desire for the Supernatural," *The New Scholasticism*, XXIII (1949), 281-317.

————. "Duns Scotus and the Existence and Nature of God," *Proceedings of the American Catholic Philosophical Association*, XXVIII (1954), 94-121.

Ethics

Binkowski, Johannes. *Die Wertlehre des Duns Scotus*. Berlin-Bonn: Dümmler, 1936.

Boehner, Philotheus. "Die Ethik des Erkennens nach Duns Skotus," *Wissenschaft und Weisheit*, II (1935), 1-17.

Budzik, Gratianus. *De conceptu legis ad mentem Ioannis Duns Scoti*. Burlington, 1955.

Dev Oglu, Gregorius. *Ethica seu Ethica generalis ad mentem ven. I. Scoti D. Subtilis*. Jerusalem: Typis PP. Franciscalium, 1906.

————. *Ius naturae seu Ethica specialis ad mentem ven. I. Scoti D. subtilis. Cum triplice appendice: De quaestione sociali, feminismo et arbitratu internationali*. Jerusalem: Typis PP. Franciscalium, 1906.

Klein, Joseph. *Der Gottesbegriff des J. Duns Scotus vor allem nach seiner ethischen Seite betrachtet*. Paderborn: Schöningh, 1913.

──────. "Zur Sittenlehre des Johannes Duns Skotus," *Franzis-kanische Studien,* I (1914), 401-37; II (1915), 137-69.

──────. "Intellekt und Wille as die nächsten Quellen der sittlichen Akte nach Johannes Duns Skotus," *Franziskanische Studien,* III (1916), 309-38; VI (1919), 107-22; 213-34; 295-322; VII (1920), 118-34; 190-213; VIII (1921), 260-82.

──────. "Il primato della volontà secondo Scoto," *Rivista di filosofia neoscolastica,* XVII (1925), 204-209.

Minges, Parthenius. "Bedeutung von Objekt, Umständen und Zweck für die Sittlichkeit eines Aktes nach Duns Scotus," *Philosophisches Jahrbuch,* XIX (1906), 338-47.

Morcelloni, Ambrogio. *La legge morale in Duns Scoto.* Doctoral Dissertation. Milan: University of the Sacred Heart, 1951.

Oromí, Miguel. "Principios básicos de la Etica de Escoto," in *Métodos y Principios Filosóficos.* Madrid: Editorial Cisneros, 1960. Pp. 225-67.

Petruzzellis, Nicola. "Studi sull'etica di Scoto," *Archivio di filosofia,* X (1940), 66-87; 219-33; 390-416.

Piernicarezyk, Erich. "Das Naturgesetz bei Johannes Duns Scotus," *Philosophisches Jahrbuch,* XLIII (1930), 67-91.

Schwendinger, Fidelis. *Metaphysik des Sittlichen nach Johannes Duns Scotus.* Werl in W., 1938.

Soto, Anthony R. "The Structure of Society according to Duns Scotus," *Franciscan Studies,* XI (1951), 194-212; XII (1952), 71-90.

Stratenwerth, Günter. *Die Naturrechtslehre des Johannes Duns Scotus.* Göttingen: Vandenhoeck & Ruprecht, 1951.

Zuccherelli, Donato. "Il pensiero del b. Giovanni Duns Scoto sulla contingenza dell'ordine etico," *Studi Francescani,* 12, vol. I, (1914-15), 385-401.

Reviews where studies on Scotistic philosophy appear more frequently:

Antonianum (quarterly). Edited by the professors of the Athenaeum Antonianum de Urbe. (Rome, 1926.)

Archivum Franciscanum Historicum (quarterly). Published by the Franciscan Fathers of the Collegium S. Bonaventurae. (Quaracchi, 1908.)

Collectanea Franciscana (quarterly). Edited by the Capuchin Fathers. (Assisi, 1931; Rome, 1941.)

Estudios Franciscanos (quarterly). Edited by the Capuchin Fathers of Barcelona. (Barcelona, 1907.) Known until 1948 as *Estudis Franciscans.*

Études Franciscaines (bimonthly). Edited by the French Capuchin Fathers. (Paris, 1889.)

La France Franciscaine (quarterly). Edited by the French Friars Minor. (Paris, 1918.)

Franciscan Studies (quarterly). Published by The Franciscan Institute, St. Bonaventure University, St. Bonaventure, N. Y. (New Series, 1941.)

Franziskanische Studien (quarterly). Published by the Friars Minor. (Paderborn in W., 1913.)

Philosophisches Jahrbuch der Görres-Gesellschaft (quarterly). Founded by C. Gutberlet and J. Pohle. (Fulda, 1888.)

Rivista di filosofia neoscolastica (bimonthly). Founded by Father Agostino Gemelli. Edited by the faculty of philosophy at the University of the Sacred Heart. (Milan, 1909.)

Studi Francescani (quarterly). Edited by the Italian Friars Minor. (Florence, 1914.)

Verdad y Vida (quarterly). Published by the Spanish Franciscan Fathers. (Madrid, 1943.)

Wissenschaft und Weisheit (quarterly). Published by the Friars Minor of München-Gladbach and Salzburg. (Werl in W., 1934.)

INDEX

Abstraction, Aristotelian doctrine of, 43; difference between Aristotelian and Scotistic, 100-101; doctrine of, *95-101;* natural way of knowing things, 40

Accidents, intellect and will are not, 77

Active power, 76

Acts, *see* Indifferent acts

Aeterni Patris, encyclical, 197

Agent intellect, 95ff

Albert the Great, St., 18

Alexander of Hales, 189

Analogy, doctrine of, 33

Anselm, St., 9, 133, 134, 135, 144; *see also* Ontological argument

Aristotelianism, difference between Platonism and, 26

Aristotelian school, 15ff

Aristotelian-Thomistic metaphysics, 26

Aristotle, 17, 20, 48, 51, 52, 62, 63, 65, 86, 87, 100, 112, 113, 123, 124, 129, 149, 157, 169

Augustine, St., 9, 20, 42, 52, 102, 116, 117, 129, 169

Augustinian metaphysics, 26

Augustinian school, 15ff

Averroes, 73

Avicenna, 157

Bak, Felix, 197

Balic, Carolus, 5, 8

Barth, Timothy, 45

Being, concept of infinite, *132-33;* innatism of the idea of, 44f, 130f; intrinsic modes of, 38; intuitive knowledge of, 40; most perfect, 143; as primary and adequate object of the human intellect, 32; reason for contingent, 157ff; univocity of the concept of, *33-39; see also* Analogy; Contingent being; Infinite being; Univocity

Belmond, Séraphin, 190

Blondel, 199

Boehner, Philotheus, 194

Bonaventure, St., 9, 13, 14, 15, 16, 19, 42, 43, 81, 109, 138, 186, 187, 189, 199

Bontadini, Gustavo, 119

Brancati, Cardinal Lorenzo, 195

Caramuel, 197

Cause: equivocal efficient, 84; first efficient, *139-42;* supreme final,

215

Wadding, Luke, 2, 8, 12

Wadding's edition of Duns Scotus' works, 8

Will, arguments for primacy of, *83-86;* different conceptions of, 85; freedom of divine, 157ff; as a self-determining power, 82f

William of Ockham, 193, 194

Windelband, Wilhelm, 193

Wolter, Allan B., 138

Works of Duns Scotus, *8-14;* authentic, *9-12;* doubtful, *13-14;* unauthentic, *12-13*